# The Brontës in the Spen Valley

# The Brontës in the Spen Valley

## Mabel Ferrett

Illustrated by Stanley Chapman

Published by
Kirklees Cultural Services
Red Doles Lane
Huddersfield
HD2 1YF

First published under the title *Shirley Country*, Hub Publications, 1973
2nd edition published with the title *The Brontës in the Spen Valley*, Hub Publications 1978
3rd edition, revised and brought up to date, 1997

ISBN 0 900746 67 X

© 1997 M Ferrett

Kirklees Cultural Services are not responsible for the materials and opinions contained herein, which are the responsibility of the author.

All rights reserved. No parts of this publication may be reproduced, stored in a retrieval system, or transmitted in any form or by any means, electronic, mechanical, photocopying, recording or otherwise, without the prior permission of the Copyright Holder and the Publisher, nor circulated in any form or binding or cover other than that in which it is published and without a similar condition being imposed on the subsequent publisher.

Printed by Pennine Printing Services Limited,
Halifax, West Yorkshire.

# Contents

| | |
|---|---|
| Acknowledgements | vi |
| The Beginning of the Story | 1 |
| Adventures in Dewsbury | 9 |
| Patrick comes to Hartshead | 17 |
| Legends Galore | 23 |
| Thornton : the happiest years | 32 |
| Roe Head | 40 |
| Red House | 60 |
| Birstall | 70 |
| An Age of Governesses | 80 |
| Postscript | 87 |
| Bibliography | 93 |
| Index | 97 |

# Acknowledgements

The author would like to express grateful thanks to the following people and organisations for their help in the production of this book.

Mr Robert Chapman for permission to reproduce his father's drawings and the Brontë country map.

Mr Tom Leadley for information about Lee Fair.

Mrs Catherine Hall for information about Oakwell Hall.

Ms Helga Hughes for information on Red House

Holly Bank School, Roe Head, Mirfield.

Mrs Isobel Schofield (editor) for her skill and patience.

Mr Eric Wright (Heckmondwike) for the photograph of the author.

# The Beginning of the Story

The River Spen, from which the Spen Valley takes its name, is only nine miles long. It rises in the Wibsey Heights on the outskirts of Bradford and it flows through Hunsworth, Cleckheaton and Heckmondwike to Dewsbury, where it enters the River Calder at Ravensthorpe. This tiny river gave its name to a parliamentary borough (Spenborough) and to a parliamentary constituency.

It was in this district that the whole story began

It began in December 1809 when Patrick Brontë, tall, well built, 32 years of age, arrived at Dewsbury, where he was to be curate for approximately two years. He came wearing a blue Irish linen frock coat and he brought his shillelah with him. A shillelah, the dictionary tells us, is an oak sapling or branch of the blackthorn. It is about fifteen inches long and is the traditional cudgel of the Irishman.

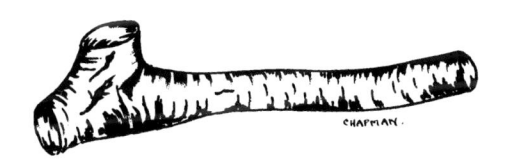

*Shillelah*

It had taken Patrick 32 years to find his way to Yorkshire. Having once arrived, he stayed, leaving the county, as far as we know, on only three occasions afterwards. The first was when he took his daughters to Cowan Bridge School, just outside Yorkshire on the road to

*Dewsbury Minster*

Kendal, and the second time was when he took Charlotte and Emily to the Pensionnat Heger in Brussels, Belgium, where they hoped to equip themselves with sufficient learning to be able to establish and run a girls' school, in England, similar to Miss Wooler's at Roe Head, Mirfield, where Charlotte, herself, had already been first a scholar and then teacher. After seeing his two daughters settled in, Patrick allowed himself a rare indulgence. The Duke of Wellington had long been his hero (as he was also Charlotte's) and so he returned home via Flanders and northern France in order to see the famous battlefield of Waterloo (1815), the memory of which was still fresh in the minds of many of his countrymen some 27 years later. Patrick recorded in his notebook that he had then visited Lille, Dunkirk and Calais, where he boarded a ferry home. He was away about two and a half weeks.

Four years after that, when he was 69 years of age, Charlotte accompanied him to Manchester for a - successful - cataract operation on the left eye.

All that was in the future, however, when Patrick arrived at Dewsbury just before Christmas in 1809, but he did leave his mark there. Even so, he would surely have been amazed had he been told that, one day, there would be a plaque to his memory on the wall of the south aisle of a church that was to become Dewsbury Minster.

Dewsbury is situated in a deep hollow in the foothills of the Pennines, and on the River Calder. It is a manufacturing town, brightened by green traffic islands and flowers, but it also has a long history. In pre-Norman days it was the centre of a parish that covered some 400 square miles and extended westwards as far as the Pennine watershed. Archaeological remains suggest that the church was, at that time, a *Minster*, i.e. a centre from which priests were sent to minister to outlying communities. There is a legend, which may well be true, that the great St. Paulinus (himself a missionary from Rome) came here in 627 A.D. when he preached, celebrated Mass and baptised his flock in the River Calder. *Hic Paulinus praedicavit et celebravit.* It is recorded that these words were inscribed on the high, richly-sculptured 9th century cross that once stood on the site. The cross has long since been broken up, but fragments have survived and are now on display in the exhibition area of the church, together with other stone fragments, one of which was discovered in 1994 - a 9th century, shaped stone, that is believed to have been part of the ancient Anglo-Saxon Minster.

*This Minster has been re-born, recently!*

*Paulinus Cross*

Extensive and imaginative improvements to the former dull Victorian-restored building have transformed it. New rooms, new staircases, new chapels, arches, iron screens and exquisite modern stained glass have been designed to blend with the old glass and ancient stones and a Minster has risen again to be an influential religious and cultural centre for Dewsbury and outlying districts.

The work is not finished yet. New precincts are to be developed in order to create a still centre in the midst of the town's noise and bustle, near enough to shops and factories for people to be able to step aside for a moment's prayer, or simply for a cup of tea in the little, welcoming Minster café.

Patrick, of course knew nothing of this when he arrived just before Christmas 1809, to take up his duties under the Vicar of Dewsbury, the Revd John Buckworth, M.A.

Used as he was to Irish clergy, Mr. Buckworth must have been a little startled by the eccentricities of his new curate. "Clever and good hearted, but hot tempered and, in fact, a little queer", was the opinion of Mr. Elliot Carrett, a Dewsbury attorney. "Old Staff" his fellow clergymen, the Revd T. Atkinson and the Revd Hammond Roberson used to call him. They could have found a worse name.

But Patrick and his vicar were soon firm friends. The Revd John Buckworth was two years younger than Patrick. He was also a writer. He wrote the hymn,

*Great God and wilt Thou condescend*
*To be my Father and my Friend -*

Patrick had fallen on his feet.

Patrick lodged at the vicarage for a time. Later he was to lodge at the Ancient Well House in Priest Lane, now Church Street. Sundays apart, he had most of his meals alone in his study. It is said that he lived almost entirely on oatmeal porridge and dumplings. He would have a week's supply of dumplings made at a time. His vicar would often remonstrate with him and urge him to keep a better table, but in vain.

The vicarage where Patrick lodged was pulled down in 1889 and the site, together with the garden and enclosure, is now part of the churchyard and adjoining road.

At the time of the demolition the shell of the building was thought to be 250 to 300 years old, but the interior was older still. According to W.W. Yates, author of *The Father of the Brontës*, published in 1897, the interior walls "except where restoration had taken place, were constructed of oak logs, with wattle and daub, the whole lined with wainscotting of the same wood". It was the oldest house in Dewsbury.

Nevertheless, it was a comfortable house. On the ground floor it had an entrance hall, a drawing room with a large fireplace and ingle nook, a dining room, a breakfast room and Mr. Brontë's 'den', which had once been the butler's pantry. This pantry was sometimes called the pump-room. It had a pump to which neighbours would come to fetch water for a special treat; it was so good for tea-making they said.

The water probably did have an unusual tang. It had drained into the well below the pump from a graveyard that, for more than 500 years, had been the only burial place for the townships of Dewsbury, Soothill and Ossett.

No wonder the vicarage was said to be haunted by a lady in green!

The Dewsbury register books show that Patrick officiated for the first time in Dewsbury at the marriage of John Senior and Ellen Popplewell on 11 December 1809. It was said of him that he was "of the evangelical school". It may well be that he was influenced by John Wesley himself. The Revd Thomas Tighe, who had coached Patrick for entry into university, was a friend of Wesley. John Wesley used to stay with Tighe whenever he was near him on his preaching tours.

At Dewsbury Patrick was considered to be a serious man, not so good a preacher as his vicar - in those days he preached with a markedly Irish accent – but one who did good work in the town as well as within the organisation of the church. There was still much of the teacher in him. He would catechise the children once a month, scholars from the Wesleyan Sunday School as well as his own.

The Sunday School in Dewsbury is believed to be one of the oldest in the country. A school was started there in 1783, three years after Robert Raikes started the school at Gloucester which developed into a national movement for Sunday Schools. The Dewsbury school was started by the Revd Hammond Roberson, who later was to serve as a prototype for the Revd Matthewson Helstone, Caroline's uncle, in Charlotte Brontë's novel *Shirley*. It is said that Mr. Roberson taught up to 300 or 400 children - not in one building, but in cottages scattered through his parish. The cottagers were paid one shilling each Sunday for the use of their rooms.

In 1883 a medal was struck to celebrate the Centenary of the Dewsbury Sunday School. On it are the easily recognised portraits of the Revd Hammond Roberson and the Revd John Buckworth with their initials H.R and J.B. beneath them.

So it was a flourishing Sunday School that Patrick Brontë inherited at Dewsbury and Patrick proved himself no mean successor to Mr. Roberson. He taught reading and writing as well as religious instruction. He, too, enjoyed holding cottage meetings but not just for children. It is said the mere phrase "Mr. Brontë is here," would fill the kitchen or "house" as the living room always used to be called in Yorkshire in those days.

# Adventures in Dewsbury

The Revd Patrick Brontë had a winning way with children and grown-ups alike. Two incidents in Dewsbury made him a hero among them. The first was when he saved a child from drowning in the River Calder.

It was winter and there had been a good deal of rain so the river was full. A group of boys, one of them of abnormally low intelligence, were amusing themselves by trying to fish floating pieces of wood from the water. Eventually they grew tired of the game and turned their attention to the half-wit, teasing and pushing him as boys do. Suddenly there was a shout and a scream as the boy fell into the river.

It was lucky for that boy that a tall gentleman, who had just passed the group, heard the scream and came running back. He jumped into the river, seized the lad and struggled with him to the bank. It was said by the boys who watched that it looked as though the gentleman could not swim.

Once out of the water, they realised that the rescuer was Mr. Brontë, the curate. They followed him sheepishly as, wet-through himself, he carried the half-drowned boy home to his mother, a widow at Dawgreen. When he came out of the cottage he stopped and lectured the boys.

"I only picked him to mak him wet his shoon", the chief culprit explained.

His penance was to go and apologise to the child and the child's mother.

The second incident was that of the Whitsuntide Sing.

It was the custom in those days for the scholars and teachers of the Sunday School to walk in procession through the main streets of the town every Whit Monday or Tuesday and then make their way through what is now known as the Dewsbury Cutting, up to Earlsheaton, where the "sing" would take place in the centre of the village, the Town's Green. This continued until 1829, by which time Earlsheaton had its own church and Sunday School.

The road out of Dewsbury was said to be a Roman road. Even today it is steep. Double-decker buses crawl up it in low gear. In those days it would be rougher, narrower and steeper in places.

*Dewsbury Cutting*

This particular Whit Tuesday in 1810 Mr. Buckworth, the Vicar of Dewsbury, was too unwell to climb the hill, so it was Patrick who was in charge. The girls were leading the procession and they had just turned off from the Wakefield road and were walking along the road to Earlsheaton when, to quote W.W. Yates, "a tall, lusty man, seeing them approach, deliberately planted himself in their path and would not move an inch. Mr. Brontë, seeing this, walked quickly up and, without a word, seized the fellow by the collar and by one effort flung him across the road and then walked by the procession to the Town's Green as if nothing unusual had happened, leaving the obstructionist agape with surprise".

The bully, it was discovered later, came from Gawthorpe, near Ossett. He was a notorious boxer and cockfighter and was very fond of the bottle.

"We talked about it for many a Sunday," a Mr. Senior used to tell in later life. He had been a boy in the procession at the time. "What sort of teacher was Mr. Brontë?" W.W.Yates asked him. "He was resolute about being obeyed," came the reply, "but was very kind and we always liked him".

Patrick, too, must have talked about the Whitsuntide Sing in later life. He must have told the story to Charlotte, because she used it in her book *Shirley*, where the Revd Matthewson Helstone meets obstructing dissenters.

Matters did not always work out so smoothly, however. There was his tiff with the bell-ringers. It was Sunday evening and the following day there was to be a bell-ringing contest with teams from other towns.

The vicar, the Revd John Buckworth, was away from home, and while the cat is away the mice will play. After evensong the ringers decided they would be able to have one last practice, undisturbed.

They had reckoned without Patrick. Bell-ringing for such a purpose was - to him - a desecration of the Sabbath and he would not allow it. Seizing his shillelah, he rushed to the church tower, stopped the ringing and drove the astonished offenders from the tower.

Next morning an indignant group of campanologists turned up at the vicarage to complain. They had done their duties for the day, they said. Why could they not have an hour's practice? But Patrick was adamant; so adamant that one bell-ringer refused to enter the bell-tower again until Patrick had apologised. Patrick lost a bell-ringer.

But the affair of William Nowell of Dawgreen, Dewsbury, wrongly imprisoned as a deserter from the army, had a happier ending.

Britain was at the time in the middle of a long, weary war with Napoleon. To keep up the supply of soldiers, recruiting officers were sent round the local fairs to offer a "recruiting shilling" to any likely lad who was willing to enlist. The passing of the shilling was all-important. Once a man had accepted it, he was under orders.

It was September 1810, the time of the Latter Lee Fair at Woodkirk, West Ardsley, Wakefield. Woodkirk, today, is an expanding modern village. During the Middle Ages it was an important place. The Black Canons of Nostell Priory had a small monastery there and had been granted a Charter by King Henry I to hold two three-day Fairs, one in August and one in September. Woodkirk Fair (Lee Fair) survived the dissolution of the monasteries and is now believed to be the oldest Charter Fair in England. It derived its present name from a Dr. Thomas Leigh who, after the Dissolution, bought Nostell Priory and its estates from King Henry VIII.

Woodkirk Fair was a 'woollen' fair in the Middle Ages, famous throughout Europe, so that merchants came to it from France, Northern Italy, Spain, Germany and the Netherlands. The gypsies did not arrive until the sixteenth century but, as the trade in cloth declined, due to the rise of Wakefield as a staple town, the Lee Fairs developed into genuine gypsy fairs; horse fairs. In 1996 some 300 horses were brought there, ranging from Shetland ponies upwards. There were stalls as well, of course, selling all things of interest to horse-lovers and gypsies: saddle-ware, clothing, pots and pans, Crown Derby tea-set that gypsies love, mirrors and - still trading his traditional wares - there is usually a 'peg-man'. One aspect, though, that does make these Lee Fairs different from many other gypsy events is that Gadje are welcomed, too.

Woodkirk has one more claim to fame, especially among lovers of literature. It was here, in a monastic cell, that some of the famous Wakefield Mystery Plays were, if not actually written, at least copied out and brought into some sort of shape, for the plays themselves are by many authors and were written over a period of something like a hundred years. When they were put up for sale in 1814, along with other Townley books and MSS, they were described as belonging to the "Abbey of Widkirk, near Wakefield".

Returning to the story of young William Nowell, it was as though some irrational nightmare had engulfed him. Soldiers appeared one day out of the blue to arrest him for having failed to report at regimental headquarters at Wakefield. They accused him of having accepted the King's Shilling at the Latter Lee Fair. They would not listen when he protested that, though his father and mother had been to the fair, he himself had stayed at home all day and he could prove it. A soldier, James Thackray, a fellow townsman, declared he had formally enlisted him. That was enough. William Nowell was taken to Wakefield, charged and clapped into Wakefield gaol as a deserter.

Luckily for William Nowell, a large number of people had seen him in Dewsbury at the time he was said to have been at the Lee Fair, accepting his enlistment shilling - and under very unusual circumstances.

It was a double tragedy that, in the end, saved William Nowell. On 2 August a Dewsbury druggist had been to Rothwell to visit a friend in gaol. It had been a merry meeting and, returning home drunk, the thought had struck him that it would be a good idea to ride his horse into a place of worship where a service was being held, disturbing the minister and congregation. For this exhibition of high spirits he was committed to Dewsbury gaol, then known as Old Towser.

His wife, who was pregnant, was so upset by the news that she was brought prematurely to labour and died in childbirth. This consequence of his foolishness so troubled the druggist that he, too, fell ill and died. He was buried nine days after his wife, on 14 August.

That however, was not the end of the matter. Lying tongues began to spread the rumour that he had died of poison. Eventually the body was exhumed, examined, declared to be free from poison and then re-interred.

The exhumation took place on the day of the Latter Lee Fair and William Nowell was in the churchyard along with other friends and acquaintances to see the body lifted.

Because of the outcry raised by the Revd Patrick Brontë and other eminent townsmen, William Nowell was eventually set free, but only after he had spent ten undeserved weeks in prison. The soldier, James Thackray, was indicted for perjury, found guilty and sentenced to seven years transportation. Then the Revd Patrick Brontë received the following letter from no less a person than Lord Palmerston,

*WAR OFFICE, 5th December, 1810.*
*Sir*
*Referring to the correspondence relative to William Nowell, I am to aquaint you that I feel so strongly the injury that is likely to arise to the Service from an unfair mode of recruiting, that if by the indictment which the lad's parents are about to prefer against James Thackray they shall establish the fact of his having been guilty of perjury, I shall be ready to indemnify them for the reasonable and proper expenses which they shall bear on the occasion.*
*I am, sir,*
*Yours, &c.,*
*(signed) PALMERSTON*

*To the Reverend P. Bronte, Dewsbury, near Leeds.*

Because of work like this it should be no surprise that, when Patrick's fiery temper got the better of him again, his friendly vicar forgave him. This was towards the end of his stay in Dewsbury. It was Sunday and Patrick had spent the morning and afternoon at Hartshead, taking services there. Usually after that he would have nothing to do at Evensong at Dewsbury, apart from reading some of the prayers, but the vicar had asked him if, this time, he would take the entire service for him as it was a special family occasion and he wanted to spend the evening with his wife's relatives, the Hallileys. Patrick promised to do this.

However, a thunderstorm broke out as he was riding home from Hartshead and Patrick arrived at Dewsbury drenched to the skin. There was not much time for changing, so he made for the Halliley's, met Mr. Halliley, explained what had happened and begged Mr. Buckworth to officiate instead.

"What?" exclaimed Mr. Halliley, probably in joke, "Keep a dog and bark himself?"

That evening a cool and collected Mr. Brontë announced before the sermon that, as he had been grievously insulted, this would be the last sermon he would preach from that pulpit.

And it was!

However, there was no break in friendship between Patrick and his Vicar. Both men were too sensible for that and soon afterwards Patrick moved to Hartshead.

# Patrick comes to Hartshead

The church to which Patrick came to officiate in 1810, but to which he was not officially inducted until 20 July 1811, was an old one. Mrs. Gaskell, writer of the first biography of Charlotte Brontë, gave an excellent description of the place: "from its high situation," she wrote "- on a mound as it were, surrounded by a circular basin - commanding a magnificent view".

In prehistoric times that circular basin was the site of a glacial lake. Geologists call it Lake Calderdale. Waters of the River Calder and some of its tributaries drained into it. Prehistoric man made his home on the hillside above the lake; e.g. at places like Norristhorpe, near Heckmondwike, where a stone age axe-head was found in 1907, 4½ inches long with a cutting edge of 2 inches. It had been ground and polished and may have been in use some 3,000 years ago.

Castle Hill at Almondbury, on the other side of the circular basin from Hartshead, must have been a familiar sight to Patrick Brontë although he never saw the tower that crowns the hill. That was erected in 1898 to commemorate Queen Victoria's Jubilee.

The site is that of a major hill-fort, timber-laced and with vitrified ramparts, dating back possibly to the Bronze Age, certainly to the Iron Age. The fort has been carefully excavated now and one theory that had been long held - that it had been the headquarters of the Brigantian Queen Cartimandua who betrayed Caratacus to the Romans - has now been exploded. The fort was abandoned some time during the fourth century B.C. and was not occupied again until the Middle Ages. Sometime during the fifth and sixth centuries B.C. it was fired, probably by enemy action and the oak ramparts that had been constructed burned so hotly that the defences vitrified; the siliceous stone walls that supported the ramparts were turned to glass.

*Castle Hill*

How much of all this did Patrick know? Something, certainly. Charlotte describes Kirklees (about a mile from Hartshead Church),

> " - *Nunnwood, the sole remnant of antique British forest in a region whose lowlands were once all sylvan chase, as its highlands were breast-deep heather -*"

The Romans, too came to Hartshead. Two Roman roads met on Hartshead Moor and they are marked on the West Yorkshire Archaeological Survey Map, No. 9, of Roman West Yorkshire, (1981). One was part of the Manchester/York road (Margery 712) that passed through Slack where there was a Roman fort that has been excavated, yielding pottery and tiles. After that the road crossed the River Calder south-east of Brighouse and continued, presumably through Cleckheaton, Leeds and on to Tadcaster. Another possible road ran from Wakefield, via Street Side at Ossett, through Dewsbury, down to Heckmondwike, crossing the River Spen by means of a ford, then up to Hightown, joining Margery 712 on Hartshead Moor. We also know that the Romans smelted iron at Low Moor, Bradford, four miles as the crow flies from Hartshead Church.

After the Romans left Britain this area became part of the Kingdom of Elmet. Elmet was a little Celtic kingdom which held out against the invading Anglo-Saxons for a hundred years after the rest of Yorkshire had been subjugated. It fell at last in 616 A.D. after which the Angles invaded and settled, and names still survive that end in *ton* (a farmstead, or enclosure), or *ley* (a meadow ), or *shaw* (a small wood), that show where they made their homes.

In the end there were more invaders than original inhabitants who, themselves, were now considered to be the foreigners. The Angles called them *walsh* which means foreign and this term is preserved in the name Walton Cross - the cross at the farmstead of the foreigners. The base of this Anglo-Saxon cross is still there. The complete structure would stand 15 feet high and it was probably coloured. In the church at Burnsall, in Wharfedale, there is a fragment of a cross of this period that still retains its original colouring - red. Erected on the edge of the escarpment, Walton Cross would be a wonderful and welcoming sight to the traveller making his way north from the sparsely inhabited countryside where Huddersfield is now.

Patrick would certainly have known about the cross. It was erected around 1,000 A.D. about a quarter of a mile from the church. Why? No one knows. It could have been a preaching cross or a boundary stone, or both. In the twelfth century it was known as the *Wagestan*.

There is no mention of a church at Hartshead in the Doomsday Book, but the mention of Kirklees (i.e. Church Meadows) suggests there was a church of some sort there before the Conquest. Although the church has been rebuilt since his day (in 1881), Patrick would be familiar with the two Norman arches that are still preserved. They are the Chancel arch and the archway over the inner door. The outer arch of the porch is a modern imitation. The old font basin, dated 1662, is made from the drum of one of the Norman pillars. Opposite the gate of the church there are mounting steps and the posts for stocks.

Patrick would also know the old yew tree in the churchyard. Possibly planted at the first building of the church as a sign of consecration, it may have provided branches for the bowmen of Hartshead at the time of Agincourt and Crécy.

Patrick was 34 years old when he was inducted at Hartshead cum Clifton. In moments of sickness or depression he probably felt much of his life had slipped by without his making very much of it.

*Old Church Hartshead
as it was in the time of Patrick Brontë*

Patrick however was only just coming into his own. The really creative years still lay ahead; the happiest years of his life.

He had a little more leisure now. He had no school to follow. A free grammar school had been founded in the district in 1729 by Sir John Armytage, Bart. of Kirklees Hall. The schoolmaster was often the curate, but Patrick was not given the post.

Nor did he know - at that time - the little Sunday School building that stands in the churchyard, near the roadside. That was not built until 1828.

There was no vicarage either, so Patrick lodged at Thorn Bush Farm, or Lousy Thorn Farm as it was sometimes called. He was looked after by Mr. and Mrs. Bedford, who had both been in service at Kirklees Hall and knew how to make a gentleman comfortable.

It was while he was at Thornbush Farm that Patrick became an author. His *Cottage Poems* were published in 1811, *The Rural Minstrel* followed in 1813, *The Cottage in the Wood* in 1815 by which time Patrick was Minister at Thornton and here, for the first time, the diaeresis was used above the *ë* in his name. *The Maid of Killarney,* Patrick's novel or "modern tale" as he called it, "in which are interwoven some cursory remarks on religion and politics" was published in 1818.

Patrick however was no writer. He was intelligent, but he lacked the facility for both poetry and fiction. He was a practical man. His best attempts at verse show this,

*The latch I gently raised,*
*And ope'd the humble door;*
*An oaken stool was placed*
*On the neat sanded floor.*

and, a little further on,

*I sing of real life.*

It may have been this inherited longing to sing of "real life" that, a generation later, was to make his daughter, Charlotte describe her heroine, *Jane Eyre*, as "disconnected, poor and plain".

# Legends Galore

While he was living at Hartshead Patrick must have visited Kirklees Hall and Park. Charlotte certainly did so for she describes the house in *Shirley*. But did either of them, one wonders, believe the legends of Robin Hood that still cling to the place?

Charlotte called Kirklees Park "Nunnwood", for there was a nunnery there in olden days.

Kirklees Priory was founded in the twelfth century by Reiner le Fleming, who held land at Hartshead and Clifton. Its nuns wore a white tunic or robe, with a black scapular and girdle. Lay sisters wore darker colours. The Cistercians were farmers. By the thirteenth century they had won a name for themselves as exporters of wool. The nuns, too, often worked the fields

*Dumb Steeple*

Kirklees was a small priory - the chapel seated only 22 nuns - but it carried with it the privilege of sanctuary. The Dumb Steeple, a monument at the junction of the Leeds-Huddersfield and Brighouse-Huddersfield roads, is supposed to have been the "Doom Steeple" originally, i.e., perhaps the place to which a doomed man, fleeing from justice, might come for safety.

Was it, one wonders, "sanctuary" that Robin Hood sought, as well as medical aid, from his relative, the prioress?

Was there a Robin Hood?

J.C. Holt, Professor of Medieval History at the University of Cambridge, suggests it "is more likely than not" that there was a real person, an original, behind all the legends, even though many of the stories that accrued are minstrels' tales. If so, this person was probably active around the year 1323 when Edward II's northern progress took place, between April and November, and King and outlaw met in the forest and made their peace. Robin Hood was a yeoman and could have been born in Wakefield for there are Hoods recorded in the Wakefield Court Rolls as early as 1274. Legends abound, though. Shakespeare knew them. In the *Second Part of Henry IV* he wrote facetiously:

*Falstaff:*         Let King Cophetua know the truth thereof.
*Justice Silence:* And Robin Hood, Scarlet and John.

and, later, Charlotte Brontë:

*The Gatehouse, Kirklees, 1973*

*"And that," asked Miss Keeldar, pointing to the forest - "that is Nunnwood?"*
*"It is."*
 ....
*"Was it not one of Robin Hood's haunts?"*
*"Yes, and there are mementoes of him still existing."*

The most persistent legend, locally, is the story of how Robin Hood met his death. Falling ill, he came to the tiny Nunnery at Kirklees where a relative of his was Prioress, "very skylful in physique and surgery", but she did not try to heal him; instead she bled him to death.

Lodged in the Priory Gatehouse and feeling himself growing weaker, Robin Hood summoned Little John.

*Robin Hood's Grave, Kirklees*

"Bring me my bow", he ordered, "and prop me up". Then, summoning his last ounce of strength, he shot an arrow through the open window. "Bury me", he commanded, "where that arrow has fallen".

Sadly, Nikolaus Pevsner, in his *Buildings of England*, argues that the part of Kirklees Gatehouse that survives is largely post-Reformation. Of course, there may have been an earlier building on the same site but, if so, no traces have been found and Robin had died long before the present gatehouse was erected.

Robin's grave - if such it is - lies about 600 yards from the Gatehouse. There is a low wall inset with railings around it to protect the gravestone because chippings from it used to be valued as charms against toothache!

The epitaph, that dates only from the middle of the eighteenth century, reads,

*Hear underneath dis laitl stean*
*Laz robert earl of Huntingtun*
*Ne' er arcir ver az hie sa geud*
*An pipl kaukd im robin heud*
*sic utlaws az hi an iz men*
*Vil england nivr si agen*
   *Obiit 24 ('r.14) Kal. Dekrembris 1247*

But in Gough's *Sepulchral Monuments*, Vol. 1, there is a picture of a different stone. It is plain, with a raised cross botonny on a Calvary of three steps.

The Priory was closed at the time of the Dissolution of the monasteries in 1539. All the nunneries at that time were small. There were no more than 1,500 to 2,000 nuns in the whole of the country. Dame Jane Kepast, the last Prioress at Kirklees, went with four other nuns to live at Mirfield. They were granted an annual pension - the Prioress £2, the ex-nuns £1-13-4d. a year each.

After passing through various hands between 1540 and 1565 the site of Kirklees was eventually sold to John Armytage of Farnley Tyas.

How much did Charlotte know? A great deal apparently. Towards the end of Shirley, in the chapter called "THE FIRST BLUE-STOCKING" (i.e. Shirley, herself) Charlotte writes,

*The village of Nunnely has been alluded to; its old church, its forest, its monastic ruins. It also had its Hall...*

Could any description be plainer?

History and legend enough for one small place. Patrick, one imagines, would have been amazed to have been told that it was his family's destiny to become an even more potent legend and attractive force. He could have no conception of what he was starting that day in 1812 when - a school inspector now! - he set off from Hartshead to inspect scholars at Woodhouse Grove School, Apperley Bridge, near Bradford.

Patrick had visited Woodhouse Grove with his old friend, William Morgan. Woodhouse Grove had been bought by the Methodist Conference and inaugurated as an academy for the sons of Wesleyan ministers. William Morgan, like Patrick, had Wesleyan friends and connections. More important, he had lately become engaged to the daughter of the headmaster at Woodhouse Grove School, Miss Jane Fennell.

The world knows the story of what followed. Jane Fennell's, cousin, Maria Branwell, was up from Cornwall, visiting her relations and her slight figure and small roguish face, her teasing, her fun, her light-heartedness -  and, perhaps too, an underlying sadness for she had lost both her parents - all took Patrick by storm. She was twenty-nine, he was thirty-five. They were both ready for marriage. It was a lightning courtship. Patrick proposed in the grounds of Kirkstall Abbey, and they were married at Guiseley Parish Church on 29 December 1812. It was a double wedding. Jane Fennell married William Morgan, Maria Branwell married Patrick. The clergymen performed the ceremonies for each other. It was a very happy occasion and was reported in the *Gentleman's Magazine* for 1813.

*Lately, at Guiseley, near Bradford by the Revd. W. Morgan, minister of Bierley, Revd. P. Brontë, B.A., minister of Hartshead-cum-Clifton, to Maria, third daughter of the late T. Branwell, Esq. of Penzance. At the same time, by the Revd. P. Brontë, Revd. W. Morgan to the only daughter of Mr. John Fennell, headmaster of the Wesleyan Academy, near Bradford.*

Nor is it insignificant that some forty years later his by then famous daughter, Charlotte, was to end her book *Shirley* with a double wedding.

*Extracts from the parish registers recording the baptism of Maria Brontë on 23 April 1814*

After the wedding Patrick brought his bride home to the tall, three-storeyed house he had rented at the top of Clough Lane, Hightown, about a mile from the church. It was there that his first two children were born, Maria in 1813 and Elizabeth in 1815, shortly before the family moved to Thornton. Maria was christened at Hartshead on 23 April 1814. The officiating minister was the ever-faithful friend, William Morgan.

*Patrick Brontë's house at Clough Lane*

Maria and Elizabeth were the two children who were to die tragically from tuberculosis, contracted in part through the harsh conditions at Cowan Bridge, where all Patrick's girls except the youngest, Anne, were sent to school. Patrick treated Maria as an adult. She seemed the one with a mind most like his own. She knew before she died at the age of eleven, something of what it meant to be a Tory and an Anglican, why Mr. Canning was a dangerous man, and why the Duke of Wellington and Mr. Peel needed their support, so one wonders what the child born at Hightown would have accomplished had she only lived long enough.

But Maria must never have remembered Hightown for she was not two years old when Patrick exchanged livings with Mr. Atkinson, vicar of Thornton.

Why did he exchange livings? It was supposed to be at Mr. Atkinson's request. The Revd Thomas King told the story afterwards - "He had a bird to catch near Hartshead". Human nature does not change much. The "bird" was a Miss Walker of Lascelles Hall, near Huddersfield. He married her soon afterwards, but Mrs. Atkinson never lived in the Brontë house at Hightown. She and Mr. Atkinson took a house at Mirfield, called "Green House", which had a pleasant garden.

This, too, was to be important for Charlotte, who always loved gardens. When she was a schoolgirl at Roe Head, not far from Hartshead but just inside the Mirfield boundary, she would visit the Atkinsons. They were her godparents and, until *Jane Eyre* was published, they were fond of her.

Mr. Atkinson remained at Hartshead as vicar until his retirement in 1866. He died four years later, aged 89, one of the very few of Patrick's friends who outlived him.

# Thornton : the happiest years

Thornton, the *Torenton* of the Doomsday Book, owed its name to the brushwood or thorn trees that once grew around the tiny village. Mrs. Gaskell, who visited the place nearly 800 years after Norman William had landed in England, was singularly unimpressed by the place. She devoted less than a page to Thornton in her four-hundred page biography. Yet the four Brontë children who achieved fame were born there. Patrick and Maria lived there for five years.

They were the happiest years of his life, Patrick was to say afterwards.

Thornton is still a small place, some four miles as the crow flies from the centre of Bradford, and eight miles from Hartshead. When Patrick moved there, the younger end of his Hartshead congregation would walk over on a Sunday evening to hear their old parson preach. As they approached Thornton they would see where the medieval villagers used to cut turf for fuel, for Thornton was "intake", enclosed land taken in from the moor. Dotted among those moors, here and there, were deep quarries that provided good building stone.

This stony landscape bred stern characters. Dissent flourished there. The church to which Patrick Brontë came probably dates back to 1587 and in its ancient churchyard both Anglicans and Nonconformists lay at peace together.

But many Nonconformists had known little peace in their lifetimes. In 1662, when the Act of Uniformity was passed, nearly 1,000 incumbents, who were unwilling to accept the liturgy or church doctrines, vacated their livings. The Conventicle Act forbade any public worship that was not Anglican. Nonconformists were harried because the government feared that their meetings would be seed-beds of sedition and rebellion.

The Nonconformists had one of their earliest chapels at Kipping, on the outskirts of Thornton. They worshipped at Kipping, but they were buried in the Thornton Churchyard. There you can still find the grave of two staunch Nonconformists, Joseph and Accepted Lister, father and son. Joseph Lister was caught in the siege of Bradford after the Battle of Adwalton on 30 June 1643, an early battle in the Civil War that gave the Royalists control over Yorkshire for a whole year. Lister told the story in his *Autobiography*. "What a change," he wrote, describing Bradford after the battle, "nothing was left to eat or drink or lodge upon, the streets being full of chaff and feathers and meal...."

But it was his son, Accepted, whom the Thornton people loved. Accepted Lister was Minister at Kipping. He was very lame, having broken both his thighs twice. For fifteen years he preached on crutches. Yet William Cudworth records that, when he consented to come to Thornton from Bingley, the people joyfully "sent 30 men and as many carts and horses and brought him and all his moveables". He died 25 February 1709. His father followed him a fortnight afterwards.

Patrick Brontë, a century later, was to live on very friendly terms with his nonconformist brethren. He was tolerant in his religious views and must have had a wicked sense of humour as well. Maria Branwell recognised that

*Thornton Old Church and New*

when she called him her "Saucy Pat" and she must have thoroughly enjoyed his way of dealing with one old lady (a dissenter), who complained she had seen Mr. Brontë shaving himself on a Sunday morning, through the chamber window which fronted the main street. He had broken the fourth commandment.

"I should like you to keep what I say in your family," Patrick told her, well knowing that within the hour it would be all over Thornton, but little guessing how the story would be preserved for posterity, "but I never shaved in all my life, or was ever shaved by anyone else. I have so little beard that a little clipping every three months is all that is necessary."

Thornton Church (the Old Bell Chapel, as it was called on account of its bell - a luxury for clockless cottages) was, like Haworth, a Chapel of Ease to Bradford Parish Church.

It was a plain dark building. On the western gable wall there was a partly obliterated inscription which read, "This chapell was builded by ... Freemason in the yeare of our Lorde 1612." Above it was another stone with the date 1587.

The church was almost rebuilt in 1756.

Patrick however must still have been dissatisfied with it for during his ministry the south side of the building was refronted, the chapel was given a new roof and a cupola was added to the tower. A board was erected inside the church telling, "This chapel was beautified 1818. P.B. incumbent".

It was in this Bell Chapel that five of the Brontë children were baptised - Elizabeth, Charlotte, Branwell, Emily and Anne.

The Old Bell Chapel has fallen into disuse. Only the west wall is still standing. The tower is on ground-level now and a fine new church has been built up the hill and across the road. Its foundation stone was laid with masonic honours. The mallet that was used was one that had done duty at the laying of the foundation stone of St. Paul's Cathedral. This new church was consecrated on 21 August 1872.

The font at which the Brontë children were baptised is preserved in the new church. The bell is in the church too. Meanwhile, down the hill in the churchyard, the visitor can still push his way into a tiny room built on to the side of the old church. This was the vestry where the registers were signed each time after the baptisms of Patrick and Maria's children.

*The old Parsonage, Thornton*
*Birthplace of the Brontë children*

    The parsonage, where Patrick and Maria lived with their six children, is still to be seen in Market Street. Market Street, however, is now a one-way street. Approaching the old Parsonage by car from the Keighley side, drive along the valley road (B6145) towards Bradford. Look out for the Baths on your left and, a little further on, the Blue Boar Public House. Almost immediately past that, still on the left-hand side, there is a sign to the Brontë birthplace. Follow the road round, continuing to bear to the left, and you will find yourself in the narrow road the Brontës knew, which was at that time the main road to Bradford. About 100 yards further on, on the right-hand side, is the house itself. A plaque to the left of the door commemorates the birth of the four famous children who were born there: Charlotte 1816, Branwell 1817, Emily Jane 1818 and Anne 1820. The house itself is not quite as they knew it, however, for the room to the right-hand side of the front door, that was the parlour, has been extended towards the street, to make a shop. There were three rooms upstairs and three downstairs. Built in 1802, it would still be fairly new when the Brontë family moved in.

There were only 23 houses in Market Street in those days and three of those were inns. The parish was a scattered one, enclosing a circle of eight or ten miles in radius. In it were hamlets such as School Green, Headley, West Scholes, Close Head and Leventhorpe.

It was a happy time for both parents, despite Maria being pregnant four times in five years. The young couple had a servant to help in the house and they engaged Nancy Garrs as nursemaid to the children.

So there was time for social life. Their greatest friends were Dr. Firth, who brought their children into the world, and his daughter, Elizabeth. Elizabeth Firth kept a diary and it is largely from her jottings - e.g. "M.C. & E. to tea" - that we know so much of what happened in those days.

Later, after Maria Brontë had died, Patrick was to propose to Elizabeth Firth, but she did not accept him.

Surprisingly, Miss Branwell came up from Cornwall to Thornton for a holiday. In spite of being, as Nanny Garrs recorded, "so cross-like an' fault-finding' - " she stayed through the Yorkshire winter. She was with Maria when her third child, Charlotte, was born. That was the following April. Elizabeth Firth recorded , "1816, April 21st -, Sunday. C. Brontë was born". But it was 28 July before Aunt Branwell went home.

Before she left Patrick presented her with a copy of his *Cottage Poems*, inscribed "The gift of the author to his beloved sister Miss Branwell as a small token of affection and esteem. Thornton, N'r Bradford. March 29th. 1816".

There were the Kayes, too - Benjamin and Mercy Kaye of Allerton Hall. It was at their house that the Brontës first met the Firths. It was there, too, that Charlotte stayed for a while after her disastrous term at Cowan Bridge. A niece of the Kayes remembered her as a very small girl, wearing a night-cap, sitting up in a great four-poster bed.

Patrick also enjoyed himself at Thornton in his special Brontë fashion. He was writing . While he was at Thornton he wrote *The Cottage in the Wood*, 1815, and *The Maid of Killarney, or Albion and Flora*, 1818. The cottage in the wood has been identified. Mrs. Ivy Holgate (*The Cottage in the Wood* B.S.T) tells how elderly people in her childhood remembered a small white cottage - not unlike cottages in Ireland - in a clearing in Shillicake Wood. They spoke of it as "Mr. Brontë's cottage in the wood" or "the cottage Mr. Brontë put into his book".

Shillicake Wood is no longer there. It was cut down during the 1914-18 war - for pit-props.

But Patrick worked as well as played. William Scruton tells a pleasant tale of how, one March day, Patrick took some 60 young people to Bradford Parish Church (now the Cathedral) to be confirmed. As they walked down Kirkgate it began to snow and Patrick grew alarmed for the well-being of his flock, so, passing the Talbot hotel, he rushed in and ordered hot dinners to be served as soon as the service should be over. The party stayed three to four hours until the snow ceased; then they went home in excellent spirits.

No wonder that when Patrick and his family moved to Haworth in 1820 Churchfolk and Dissenters alike were sorry to see him go.

The story of Thornton does not end there, however. In 1828, eight years after Patrick left, a mill owner, Simeon Townend, set up the first power looms in the Thornton district. It is recorded that there was so much prejudice against those looms that no one would work them and the first weavers had to be brought in from Lancashire. News of this would reach the Brontë family at Haworth, when Charlotte was twelve years old. Was it this that first aroused her interest in the problems of industry, eventually leading her to base her book *Shirley* on the Luddite attack on Cartwright's mill in Liversedge?

Charlotte also considered - but never wrote - a novel dealing with the Chartist movement, a movement that reached its peak in Charlotte's own lifetime. One day she walked from Haworth to Wilsden, a village 2½ miles N.W. of Thornton, to consult Francis Butterfield, Quaker and Chartist, about the project. They talked over tea. Francis Butterfield however advised her to drop the subject. It might provoke controversy, he said.

# Roe Head

Holly Bank School, Roe Head, Far Common Road, Mirfield is no ordinary school. Its work is impressive, its staff dedicated.

It is a school for young people who have severe physical disabilities and difficulties in learning, people who need specialist teaching because they develop at different rates from the average person. The aim is to equip the 5-19 year olds with sufficient skills to enable them to live independently.

At 19 years of age much has been achieved but many of these young people are still by no means ready to leave the shelter of a school that has become home to them and take their place as adult members of the community. A new venture, therefore, has been started: *Rooftops*, a specialist independence-training project for young people up to 25 years of age.

Charlotte Brontë would have been amazed and especially interested because she, too, went to school at Roe Head and she, too, had difficulties to face. Ellen Nussey, describing her first sight of her future friend, wrote, ". . . there was a silent, weeping, dark little figure in the large bay window".

Mary Taylor, who herself had literary gifts (and even wrote a novel *Miss Miles*) has left us a glimpse of how Charlotte looked when she first arrived at Roe Head after a gap of five and a half years in her schooling.

*I first saw her coming out of a covered cart, in very old-fashioned clothes, and looking very cold and miserable.... When she appeared in the schoolroom her dress was changed, but just as old. She looked a little old woman, so short-sighted that she always appeared to be seeking something, and moving her head from side to side to catch a sight of it. She was very shy and nervous, and spoke with a strong Irish accent....*

But it was Ellen Nussey who produced the phrase that described her best at that time. She said that she looked "dried-in".

Yet Charlotte was to be happy at Roe Head. She made two life-long friends there. She could not play games because she would not wear glasses and therefore could not see the ball; but she could tell stories. She did this each night after the girls had gone to bed. One night she did it to such effect that one of the girls screamed and Miss Wooler had to come running upstairs to see what was the matter.

It is strange that at first the girls thought her "very ignorant for she had never learnt grammar at all and very little geography". Indeed Miss Wooler suggested that to start with she should be put into a lower class, but Charlotte wept so much that the idea was abandoned. She was very conscious of her deficiencies though. She was conscious, too, that she had come to Roe Head with a purpose, that of fitting herself for earning a living. With this in mind she worked almost too hard. "She did not play and amuse herself in the evenings when others did," Ellen Nussey recalled in after years. She would read as long as the light lasted until her companions accused her of being able to see

*Roe Head School*

in the dark, but the hard work brought its rewards. At the end of her first half year at Roe Head Charlotte won the three main prizes.

The house itself must have held many compensations for Charlotte. Looking out from the terrace she would see almost the same view that her father had known at Hartshead, the view across Huddersfield and the Calder basin. Inside, the rooms were oak-panelled. Drawing-room, dining-room, school-room were all on the ground floor, bedrooms occupied the second floor, while the third floor housed "the ghost", a lady in a rustling silk gown.

The school was small, more like a family than a school. During Charlotte's year and a half at Roe Head there were never more than ten pupils. That worked out at approximately two pupils per teacher, for there were five Miss Woolers - or rather four and a married sister who came in to teach drawing.

The eldest, Margaret Wooler, was the headmistress. At that time she was about forty years of age, short and stout, but graceful, like a lady abbess; so Ellen Nussey remembered her afterwards. She had a quiet dignity, a genuine love of learning and she was a linguist. She had, moreover, one gift that must have been of immense value to Charlotte. She was a raconteur. Mrs. Gaskell, in her *Life of Charlotte Brontë* tells how Miss Wooler would take her pupils for long walks and regale them with tales of "this old house or that new mill, and of the states of society consequent on the changes involved by the suggestive dates of either building". The Miss Woolers did not come to Roe Head until 1830, so they were not there when the Luddites gathered in the field in front of the house (1812) prior to their attack on Rawfolds Mill, down in the valley, but there is little doubt that, by the time Charlotte arrived the following January, they would know all about it and be ready to pass on the information to their brilliant pupil.

Charlotte was confirmed while she was a pupil at Roe Head and this was probably at Liversedge Church, although no record of it has been found. We know a Confirmation service was held there on Saturday, 24 September 1831, during a tour in which the Archbishop of York consecrated new churches (of which Heckmondwike was one) and also held confirmations. At this same time, Patrick's close friend, the Revd William Morgan of Bradford, presented Charlotte with a *Book of Common Prayer* duely inscribed and dated 1831. There is some confusion, though. Years later Charlotte was to write to her publisher about the Revd Hammond Roberson, "I saw him but once - at the Consecration of a Church - when I was a child of ten years old." Yet Mr. Roberson was the incumbent at Liversedge and must have been one of the leading clergymen at the

Confirmation ceremony. Did Charlotte fail to see him there? It could be so. She was one among 267 candidates and she was notoriously short-sighted.

The most outstanding event of Charlotte's stay at Roe Head took place in May 1832 when Branwell paid her a surprise visit. He was not yet 15 years old, yet he had walked eighteen miles from Haworth just to see her. He had another eighteen miles to walk back. "I could perceive when you arrived at Roe Head that you were very much tired," Charlotte wrote to him afterwards, "though you refused to acknowledge it". Her letter gives some idea of what they talked about that day - politics and literature, the Reform Bill, Earl Grey, *Frazer's Magazine* and *Blackwood*.

Charlotte left Roe Head in June, 1832. Ellen Nussey in her *Reminiscences* tells a moving story about this.

Before she left, Charlotte said suddenly, "I should like for once to feel out and out a schoolgirl; I wish something would happen! Let us run round the fruit garden." Running, apparently, was something she never did.

But that was not the end of Roe Head for Charlotte; only the end of her happiest period there. After a relaxation of three years, on 29 July 1835, Charlotte returned to Roe Head, this time as a teacher; and this time she had Emily with her.

Emily stayed only three months, then Anne took her place. Anne stayed under Miss Wooler for two and a quarter years. Her fees were part of Charlotte's salary, a salary that seems to have been pitiably small. After clothing herself and Anne, Charlotte had nothing left.

Moreover she missed the companionship of her friends. Anne, four years her junior, was now in the opposite camp. She was a pupil. Unable to write, Charlotte turned to religion, but found little comfort there. "If Christian perfection be necessary to Salvation", she wrote to Ellen Nussey, "I shall never be saved...".

Charlotte kept a journal from 1835-7, now part of the Bonnell Collection at the Brontë Parsonage Museum, Haworth. This journal was her lifeline. She poured all her rage and fury and frustration into it. "...am I to spend the best part of my life in this wretched bondage....?" she cried. Yet she could teach, given an apt pupil. "She made poetry and drawing ... exceedingly interesting to me", Mary Taylor wrote, remembering her. It was not the drudgery of teaching that nearly destroyed Charlotte. It was deprivation. Only when she could dream and write was Charlotte really alive.

Early in 1838, for family reasons, the Miss Woolers moved their school to Heald's House, Dewsbury Moor. Here Charlotte was to endure real unhappiness. Overworked herself, worried for her sister Emily, who had recently taken her first teaching post at Southowram, near Halifax, Charlotte suddenly found herself also responsible for a desperately sick invalid, her sister Anne, who was suffering from a neglected cold. After an explosive interview with Miss Wooler, who did not seem to realise the gravity of the situation (she had not endured Cowan Bridge!) Charlotte took her sister home. There Anne recovered.

But Charlotte came back to Dewsbury Moor - back to loneliness, hopelessness, nightmare. In the end she saw a doctor. He told her to go home if she valued her life and her reason. So, at the end of the spring term 1838, Charlotte left Dewsbury Moor for good.

Miss Wooler continued to be a very good friend. She had a house in the North Bay at Scarborough. When Anne was taken ill for the last time, and was virtually dying, Miss Wooler offered to have her there, but the doctor said the North Bay was too cold and bleak, so Anne went to the more sheltered part of the town, the South Bay, where she lived for only a few more days.

Miss Wooler also stepped into the breach at Charlotte's wedding. Patrick, old and peevish now, and frightened as well, suddenly refused to give his daughter away. Miss Wooler did it for him.

In spite of all their ups and downs together, Charlotte must have cared deeply for her old headmistress. According to Ellen Nussey, Miss Wooler was the prototype for Mrs. Pryor in *Shirley*.

Later two of the Miss Woolers kept a Dames' School in an old house in Spen Lane, Gomersal. Today that house is called Spen Cottage and overlooks the cricket field. In former days it was called Pruin Hall and Spen Lane was called Pruin Lane.

Miss Margaret Wooler, Charlotte's headmistress, died in 1885. She is buried in the new portion of the churchyard at Birstall.

# The Shirley Story

In the spring of 1812 Spen Valley people were enduring hard times. Why?

Firstly because England was at war. She was at war with both France and America. Because of this, the Spen Valley manufacturers of cloth found their major export markets cut off, thus they were in the position of having warehouses piled up with material they could not sell and they had no money coming in to keep their businesses going. Their men were out of work and there was no unemployment benefit in those days. There also had been a bad harvest. Yet the war went on.

Moreover, in 1812 England was at the beginning of her industrial revolution. Machinery was coming into the mills. One of the first pieces of machinery was the "shearing machine" or "cropping machine" or the "finishing machine" - different names for the same thing. These machines raised the nap on the cloth, then cropped it close, giving the cloth a beautifully smooth finish. Hitherto this had been done by hand, by the croppers. It was slow work. The number of croppers in the country was small and their work was very specialised. As the Spen Valley was a cloth-making area it was badly hit by the advent of these machines.

Because the machines worked more quickly and probably, once they were perfected, did the work better, the manufacturers were anxious to have them in their mills. The croppers, on the other hand, were just as anxious that they should not have them.

Rather than let that happen, they would break into the mills and smash the machinery. They had a great hammer that they called "Enoch", named after one of the makers of machinery. They had their songs too:

*Great Enoch still shall lead the van.*
*Stop him who dare! Stop him who can!*
*Press forward every gallant man*
*With hatchet, pike and gun!*

*Oh, the cropper lads for me,*
*The gallant lads for me,*
*Who with lusty stroke*
*The shear frames broke,*
*The cropper lads for me.*

As early as 1809 William Cartwright, who leased Rawfolds Mill, situated between Cleckheaton and Heckmondwike, had several of these machines installed. The driving force was a water-wheel in the river Spen. By 1812 he had decided that the experiment had been so successful that he would order more, but these were smashed in transit - by the Luddites - as they were being brought across Hartshead Moor.

In the Shears Inn at Hightown and in the St. Crispin Inn at Halifax the croppers discussed their plans for an attack on Cartwright's mill. It was to be an organised attack. Three to four hundred men were expected. In the event only about one hundred and fifty turned up.

On his side Mr. Cartwright had made his preparations. He had fortified the mill, and had the military brought into the district. Five soldiers slept with him each night in the

*The Shears Inn*

mill together with one or two of his men. The rest were billeted in the public houses round about. They were to come to his aid when they heard the mill bell.

The attack was planned for Saturday night, 11th April. The gathering point was to be the Dumb Steeple on the Leeds-Huddersfield road. Some met in the field in front of Roe Head School. They were armed. They marched down the hill, across the fields - to Rawfolds.

They crossed the little bridge over the Spen. They overcame two guards at the gate. They entered the mill yard.

*Rigby's Wire Works and River Spen
Site of Cartwright's Mill, Rawfolds*

Mr. Cartwright was awakened by the low growling of a dog. He woke his companions quickly and they stationed themselves at the upstairs windows.

Mellor, the leader of the Luddites, gave the order. "Hatchetmen advance!"

They battered the mill door. They shook the windows. Nothing gave. Then the shots rang out from the upper windows, and they fell back. Again they tried and again the shots rang out.

We have two accounts of what happened after that: first, the fictional one in *Shirley*; second, a factual account writen by Frank Peel in *Spen Valley: Past and Present*. It is interesting to compare the two.

First, Charlotte Brontë's in *Shirley*.

> "*To the back, lads!*" They heard a voice retort,
> "*Come round, we will meet you!*"
> "*To the Counting-house!*" was the order again.
> "*Welcome! - We shall have you there!*" was the response.

*Shirley* was first published in 1848 when Frank Peel was eighteen years old. He died in 1900. *Spen Valley : Past and Present* was published in 1893.

I quote from *Spen Valley : Past and Present*.

> "*To the back, lads*", he cries.
> The defiant voice of Cartwright is heard in reply:
> "*Come round, we'll meet you*".

and eight lines further on

> Again cries Mellor, "*To the counting-house.*"
> "*Welcome! We shall have you there,*" rings out the defiant voice once more, ...

Whether Frank Peel copied Charlotte's account or - more likely - went back to the same primary source, a contemporary report in the *Leeds Mercury* (which we do know Charlotte read) this, at least, proves beyond doubt that the Luddite attack on Robert Moore's mill in *Shirley* was

51

BRONTË HOUSE
THORNTON
BELL CHAPEL
B 6145
BRADFORD
A647
QUEENSBURY
A6038
A641
Shirley
NOT
RIVER SPEN
B6120
CLECKHEA
CHARLOTTE BRONTË
A644
HIGH SUNDERLAND
(DEMOLISHED)
- TO HALIFAX
A58
B6120
HARTSHEAD
MOOR TOP
A649
A641
A649
B6119
LAW HILL
SOUTHOWRAM
BRIGHOUSE
A643
HARTSHEAD CHURCH
GATEHOUSE
KIRKL
A644
A62
HUDDERSFIELD
DUMB STEEP
RIVER CALDER
CASTLE HILL
ALMONDBURY
RIVER COLNE
DRAWN
S.CHAPMA

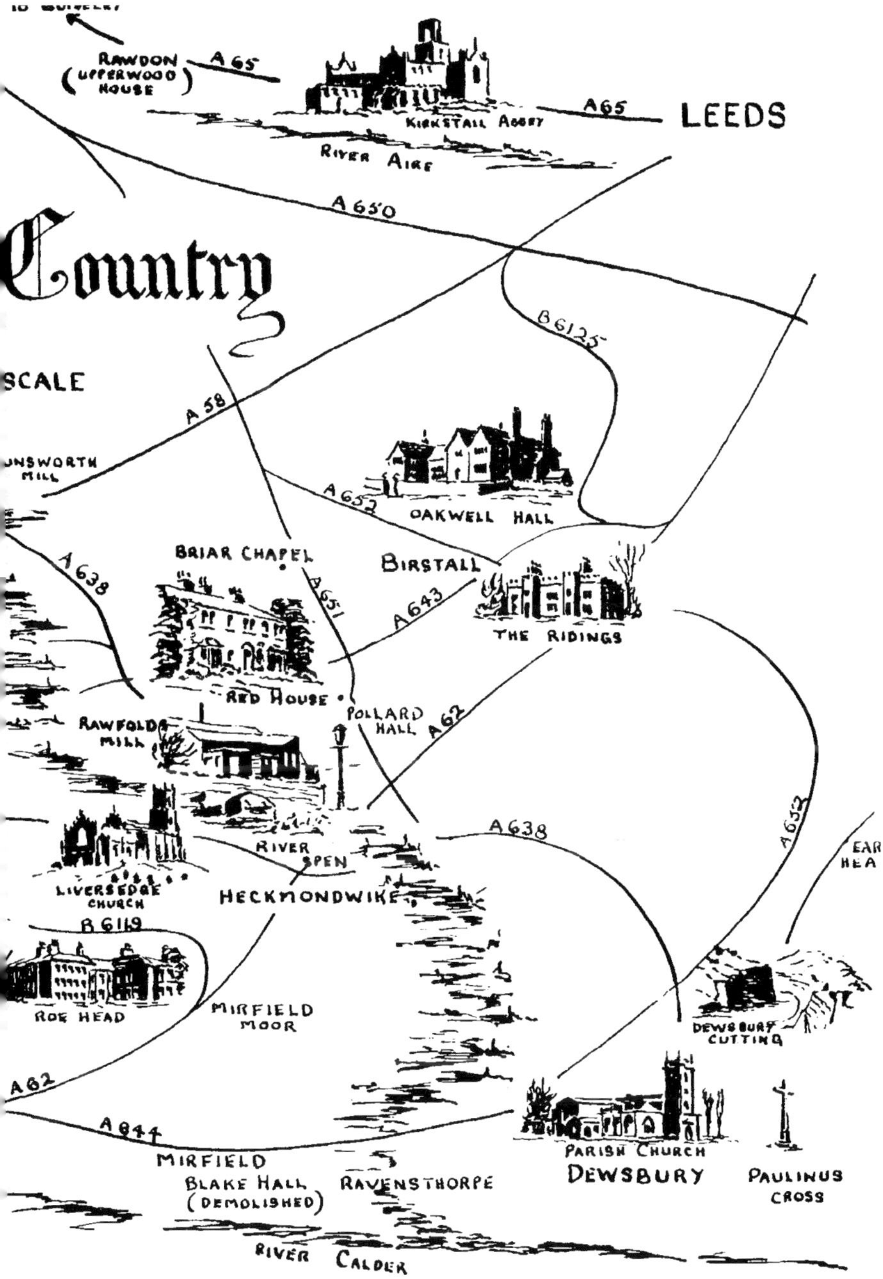

Rawdon (Upperwood House)
A65
Kirkstall Abbey
A65
LEEDS
River Aire
A650
Country
B6125
SCALE
A58
Oakwell Hall
A652
Birstall
Briar Chapel
A638
A651
A643
The Ridings
Red House
Rawfolds Mill
Pollard Hall
A62
A638
River Spen
Liversedge Church
Heckmondwike
A652
B6119
Roe Head
Mirfield Moor
Dewsbury Cutting
A62
A644
Parish Church
Mirfield
Blake Hall (Demolished)
Ravensthorpe
Dewsbury
Paulinus Cross
River Calder

based on a similar incident that took place at Rawfolds, Cleckheaton.

Finally, in the darkness the mill bell rang out summoning the soldiers who were billeted in the district. The battle raged for nearly half an hour, but in the end the rebels knew they were beaten. They fled, leaving two men bleeding and dying. Some of the Luddites fled up the hill where Royds Park is now, towards Gomersal. In the darkness they scaled a retaining wall - built to hold the soil on the hillside. It was six feet high. That wall is still called by local people "The Luddite Wall" or "Battle Wall".

Eventually, when all was quiet again, the wounded men were treated. They were removed first to the old Yew Tree Inn and then, because of the crowds, to the Star Inn at Roberttown. It was there that the militant parson, the Revd Hammond Roberson, attended them. His chief concern seems to have been how to get information from them about their accomplices and their arms caches. At last one of the men, John Booth, beckoned Mr. Roberson over to him.

*"Can you keep a secret?"*, *he gasped.*
*"Aye!" the clergyman replied eagerly. "I can!"*
*"So can I" Booth replied calmly. He would say no more.*

It was this event that Charlotte took and put at the heart of her book *Shirley*. William Cartwright became Robert Moore and the Revd Hammond Roberson, was transformed into the Revd Matthewson Helston. Charlotte remembered him as, "a personage short of stature, but straight of port, and bearing on broad shoulders a hawk's head, beak and eye, the whole surmounted by a Rehoboam, or shovel hat...."

*Charles Molyneaux*

Unfortunately this photograph cannot be authenticated now. In October 1959 I gave a talk to the Littletown Derby and Joan Club and in the course of it I told the story of Cartwright's nightly watch in the mill both before and on the night of the Luddite attack. After the talk an old lady said to me, "That story about Cartwright's men sleeping in the mill with him is true. I know it is true because my grandfather was one of those men".

I looked at her.

"1812? Your grandfather? Couldn't have been!"

She bridled. "I am 80 now," she retorted, "and when I was 3 years old my grandfather was 90. Reckon it up for yourself.

"I've got photographs of him at home," she added. "Would you like to see them?"

This is a copy of one of those photographs reproduced by her permission, given verbally, at the time. I now believe Charles Molyneaux would be about 20 years old in 1812.

This was the man who built Liversedge Church out of his own money! His portrait can be seen at the west end of the church, below the gallery.

*Heald's Hall. Home of the Revd Hammond Roberson*

The Revd Hammond Roberson came from the picturesque village of Cawston in Norfolk. He was appointed curate at Dewsbury in 1779, thirty years before Patrick Brontë. There he started what he believed was the first Sunday School in the north of England, the school which Patrick later inherited. He also won a law suit which helped to stop bull-baiting in the town. Later, like Patrick, he was curate at Hartshead (1795-1803), but his true vocation was teaching. He opened a school at Squirrel Hall, Dewsbury and in 1795 he transferred it to Heald's Hall, Liversedge. It was while he was there - after the death of his wife - that he built Liversedge Church. It cost £7,474 -11-10¾. After the consecration in 1816 he wrote to a friend, "From the best judgment I can form I am still solvent: more I have no ambition to be.... There will be a shilling left for the Sexton to level up my grave. And there is Liversedge Church".

Liversedge churchyard is quite remarkable. Almost all the gravestones are the same size and pattern. Mr. Roberson would have no other. His own gravestone can be found on the extreme edge of the churchyard, in an obscure corner. It is the same size and pattern as the others. (So are the Roberson graves in the churchyard at Cawston, Norfolk!).

But there was one man who predeceased Mr. Roberson who, even in death, managed to assert his own individuality. That was William Cartwright of Rawfolds, prototype of Robert Moore in *Shirley*. He died in 1839, two years before his friend. His is a large flat stone.

William Cartwright's mill at Rawfolds survived the attacks of the Luddites and Cartwright's fellow manufacturers presented him with three thousand pounds (and fifty guineas for the men who had helped him) and a written testimonial as a tribute to his courage. Cartwright's mill was eventually burned down. All that remains is one wall, part of Rigby's Wire Works; but the street leading to the works is still called "Cartwright Street".

As time passed the political situation eased. Trade revived. Luddism collapsed.

A strange story circulated in after years, first told, it is said by the Revd Thomas Atkinson, who succeeded Patrick

Brontë at Hartshead. Coming home late one night, past the church, Patrick heard sounds that startled him. As he watched, he realised what was happening. In this south-east corner of the graveyard, contiguous to the road, a few quiet men were burying their dead, trusting that if their parson, as a representative of law and order, could not help them, he would not betray them either.

It has been believed that the corpses were of men who had been hung at York for their parts in the Luddite attack on Rawfolds Mill. This is unlikely, although it is true that two local men were tried at the York Special Commission, January 1813.

1. John Hirst from Liversedge, cloth dresser, indicted for beginning to demolish Cartwright's Mill. He was acquitted.

2. James Starkey, Liversedge, carpet-weaver, indicted for inciting two men to blow up Cartwright's Mill. His case was put off until the next Assizes.

Both men, however, must have spent sleepless nights in gaol, never expecting justice, or mercy. Eighteen of the sixty-six Luddites who were tried were hung.

So, what really happened?

Probably the burial was of a man (or men) who had died as a result of wounds after the battle. To bury these openly, with full Church Service, would be to invite further enquiries from the authorities and possibly lead to further arrests. Patrick would realise this - and they were his flock. Besides, he himself was a poor man's son. He would understand.

In a portion of the churchyard full of memorials to the dead it is significant that there are still no tombstones in this small corner contiguous to the road.

# Red House

*Red House*

Red House, Gomersal, near Cleckheaton, was the home of Mary Taylor, Charlotte Brontë's schoolfriend.

Charlotte visited the house often and spent some of her happiest hours there. The society of the Taylors, she wrote, is one of the most rousing pleasures I have ever known.

It made such an impression on her that she put both house and family into her book *Shirley*. The house became Briarmains and the Taylor family became the Yorke family.
Despite some alterations and a pleasant addition to the

parlour at the west end, with a picture window overlooking the gardens, Red House still gives a fair impression of what it was like in Charlotte Brontë's day. This has been planned deliberately because Red House is now a Period House open to the public and the aim has been to present it as a typical home of the 1830s, together with gardens and outbuildings. These out-buildings include a barn or warehouse, dating from the days when some farming was carried on alongside the family cloth-finishing business, and coach houses, which have been fitted as exhibition galleries and are to be used for educational visits and other cultural activities. The hand-made red bricks of which the house is built suggested its name and Charlotte's descriptions of it as "Briarmains" in *Shirley* still seem extraordinarily accurate.

> *Briarmains,* she wrote, *stood near the highway, it was rather an old place, and had been built ere that highway was cut, and when a lane winding up through fields was the only path conducting to it.*

Earlier in the book Charlotte described the interior. It had "... a matted hall, lined almost to the ceiling with pictures"; In the parlour, "A series of Italian views decked the walls; ... There was a guitar and some music on a sofa; there were cameos, beautiful miniatures; a set of Grecian-looking vases on the mantelpiece; there were books well arranged in two elegant bookcases". In the back parlour were the stained glass windows, purple and amber, representing, "the suave head of William Shakespeare, and the serene one of John Milton". These windows can be seen *in situ* at Red House.

This was the home of the Yorkshire manufacturer, Joshua Taylor. Occasionally one can still meet his kind today. He was tall, had white hair, a broad forehead and a fresh complexion. There was a harshness both in his voice and features. There was also sagacity. So Charlotte described him in *Shirley*.

Mr. Taylor could speak both French and Italian and had travelled abroad. He had spent two years in Italy. This gift of tongues was thought uncanny in his native Gomersal. Perhaps that is why, when at home, he preferred to speak Yorkshire dialect. It made communication easier.

In 1840 Red House premises were described as, "house, kitchen, garden, lawn, shrubberies and plantation. Press shop, pearking shop, packing shop, counting house, coach house, cart shed, barn, stable and yard". There was also a building at the back used for cloth finishing.

The main mill however was at Hunsworth, about two miles away. This was built in 1785 by John Taylor, Mary's grandfather. Thomas Wright of Birkenshaw, who left a famous *Autobiography* behind him, recorded the event. "A friendly acquaintance of mine", he wrote, "(Mr. John Taylor, merchant of Great Gomersal) had lately built a pretty large mill for carding machines to which he had attached four stocks to mill woollen cloth". Thomas Wright became the *searcher* there; that is, he had to inspect the cloths before they were marketed and put his seal on them.

The speciality of Hunsworth Mill was the making of army cloths, known in those days as *common thick-uns*. They also made a finer cloth for export to France and Italy. The Taylors also exported to America. John Taylor did much of his own travelling in search of orders.

*Hunsworth Mill and the White Cottage (now demolished)*

This was the mill - and not Rawfolds Mill - that Charlotte Brontë described in *Shirley*. The little whitewashed cottage near the mill, where Robert Moore lived and where he proposed to Caroline has been pulled down but it was exactly as Charlotte described it.

Mary's brothers, John and Joseph, lived in Hunsworth for a while and Mary stayed with them there before emigrating to New Zealand. Ellen Nussey, in one of her letters, described how she set off from home with her youngest brother at nine o'clock one evening to visit her there. It was quite dark when they arrived. Two people (Mary Taylor and Charlotte Brontë) were out in the garden, talking. The girls approached each other cautiously, peering into each other's faces, afraid of saluting the wrong person.

Then, when they did recognise each other, an affectionate "bless you" burst forth.

Mary Taylor's grandfather was a friend of the great John Wesley. It is recorded that Wesley preached at Gomersal on 6 August 1776 and 25 August 1779. Wesley was also in the district on 28 April 1780 and 10 April 1780, when he preached to prisoners at White Lee Jail, Heckmondwike. On the first occasion the ground was covered with snow. It was six o'clock in the morning, yet so many people had gathered in the hope of hearing him that they were let into the court of the prison and John Wesley preached to them there.

John Taylor however built his own chapel, the little brick building about 200 yards below Red House on the opposite side of the road.

It presented a busy scene once. Worshippers came and stopped the greater part of the day, bringing their meals with them. Charlotte Brontë described a typical occurrence in the *Briar Chapel* or the *Ranters'* (Primitive Methodists) *Chapel* in one wonderful page in *Shirley*. There was the singing that nearly raised the roof and the cries of "I've found liberty!" "Doad o' Bill's has fun liberty!"

> *Here we raise our voices higher,*
> *Shout in the refiner's fire;*
> *Clap your hands amidst the flame,*
> *Glory give to Jesus' name!*

Fourteen people still lie buried in a little forgotten graveyard near at hand. Before the 1939-45 war one of the gravestones was dug up. The local historian, H.Ashwell Cadman, copied down the inscription.

*Isaac and Judy Smith his wife lie buried here. Judy died Dec. 1815, aged 80. Isaac died June 22. 1816 aged 84. They were among the first founders of Methodism in this County, but finding that body declining in sincerity, and the Conference seeking domination and wealth more than the Glory of God in the salvation of man, they separated from the Society, and in consequence of this exercise of superior principle they were neglected and insulted by the Pharisees of the age.*

But John Taylor is not buried there. He lies in a beautiful, secluded little burial ground in Firdene Wood, (Scotland Wood in those days). He was the first to be buried there.

*Johannes Taylor*
*Obiit 23 Dec: 1805*
*Aetatis 69*
*Regurgam*
His wife lies with him.

Joshua Taylor (Hiram Yorke) who died 28 December 1840 is there, too, with Anne, his wife . Then comes Joshua, his son, (Matthew in *Shirley* ) The cortège made its way through fields and not by road.

The last burial was that of Richard Waring, second son of Richard Waring and Edith Taylor of Red House, Gomersal, who died 14 April 1908, aged 10 months.

*The Taylor Graves, Firdene Wood, Gomersal*

It was Joshua Taylor, Mary's father, who established the "Gomersal Bank". Joshua even issued his own bank notes.

The building was in the grounds of the house. The safe was under the floor and it had walls four feet thick. The doors opened upwards. Nobody but the owners could draw the bolt, for they alone knew the secret. They used a powerful magnet. But the bank failed in 1826, a bad year for the British economy, and several thousands of pounds were owing. Joshua's son, also a Joshua (Matthew in *Shirley*) spent the next thirty years of his life working to pay off the debt.

Mary Taylor (Rose in *Shirley*) believed passionately that women should work and stand on their own feet. She emigrated to New Zealand in 1845. There she opened a shop and Charlotte sent her £10 to help her establish herself. Ellen Nussey sent her dresses and other small things.

Mary was still in Wellington, New Zealand, when *Shirley* was published and Charlotte sent her a copy. Reading it made her homesick. She wrote back "I have not seen the matted hall and painted parlour windows so plain these five years". She thought Charlotte had caught the likenesses very well. "You made us all talk much as I think we should have done". Only her father she thought was "not like ... he is not honest enough", she wrote. Nevertheless, she thought *Shirley* a better novel than *Jane Eyre*. "All through this last novel there is so much more life and stir that it leaves you more to remember than the other."

There was just one criticism. In *Shirley*, the hero, Robert Moore, is shot by the Luddites. He is brought to Red House to be nursed back to health. But Mary was surprised at one thing. Charlotte had put him in the servant's bedroom!

Mary's mother did not like the novel. Mary wrote from New Zealand, "Mama has written to Waring abusing Miss Brontë for writing *Shirley* and Waring thereupon asked to read it".

Mary Taylor made good in New Zealand. By 1860 she was able to return with a small fortune, but Charlotte was dead by then and was never to know that Mary, herself, had a novel published in 1890 - *Miss Miles: a Tale of Yorkshire Life Sixty Years Ago*. The plot was set in, and around Birstall, Charlotte Brontë's Briarfield.

Mary built a home for herself, High Royd (now High Rising) off Spen Lane, Gomersal, nearly opposite Pruin Hall, where the two Miss Woolers were to keep their Dames' school. She died there in 1893, 76 years of age and was buried, not in the family graveyard in Firdene Wood, but in Gomersal Churchyard.

Gomersal has one more - tenuous - link with Charlotte. The property next to Red House (it can be seen plainly from the front door) is Pollard Hall. Pollard Hall was the home of Herbert Knowles, the poet. He came when he was six years old, after the death of his mother, to live with his aunt and uncle, Sarah and William Burnley.

As Charlotte was to do some twenty years later, Herbert Knowles, while still at school at Richmond, sent a long poem *A Richmond Tale* (1,574 lines) to Robert Southey, the poet laureate, hoping he would help him get it published because the funds would help pay for him to go to university. The poem was not published, but Southey was so impressed by it that he arranged with friends that the money should be raised. Sadly, only two months after writing to Southey, Herbert Knowles was dead. He died at Pollard Hall. He was nineteen years old.

One poem Herbert Knowles wrote has lived. It is called *Lines written in the Churchyard of Richmond, Yorkshire* and is based on an extract from the Bible, Matthew XVII, verse four.

"*To whom shall we build a tabernacle?*" Knowles asks. *To ambition, beauty, pride, riches? No!*

*Unto Death? to whom Monarchs must bow,*
*Ah no! for his empire is known,*
*And here there are trophies enow;*
*Beneath the cold dead and around the dark stone*
*Are the signs of a sceptre that none may disown.*

In the end he builds three tabernacles - to Hope, to Faith and "to the Lamb of the great sacrifice".

One wonders did somebody in the Taylor family read the poem to Charlotte on one of her visits? Was it here she, herself, conceived the idea of writing to Robert Southey for help and advice? But Southey was 62 by this time. Besides, Charlotte was a woman. All he did was invite her to visit him if she ever found herself in the Lake District.

# Birstall

Johnson had his Boswell. In much the same way our understanding of Charlotte Brontë would be diminished were it not for Ellen Nussey. Ellen kept all Charlotte's letters (more than 400) although Charlotte's husband, the Revd Arthur Bell Nicholls, realising their intimate nature and their potential market value, insisted she should destroy them. Ellen lived long enough to see Arthur Nicholls's premonitions come true. Charlotte's letters did become valuable, but Ellen first had the good sense to put them into the eager hands of Mrs. Gaskell.

Ellen was living at Rydings (no definite article at Ellen's request!) when Charlotte first visited her. Ellen's father was dead. Her brother, John, rented the house from their Uncle Reuben, so that Mrs. Nussey and her family (she had 12 children) still had a gracious home.

That first visit took place in September 1832, some three months after Charlotte left Roe Head as a pupil. She was 16. Branwell, a year younger than his sister, escorted her there in the Haworth gig. He stayed some hours. When he went he told Charlotte he was surely leaving her in Paradise.

Rydings was very different in those days. Now it is so hemmed in with factories that it can only just be seen from the road - the Huddersfield-Leeds road, A62. The entry is the last one before the traffic lights at Birstall Smithies. Huge gates bar the entrance and there is always a man on

*Rydings, Birstall Smithies*

guard. But Yorkshire hospitality is still the rule. The Brontë enthusiast is usually allowed to go in and take photographs.

Rydings was built in the early eighteenth century, long before the A62 was cut through its park. Its title deeds go back to the time of Edward IV.

Ellen's family on both sides was *county*. The Nusseys and the Walkers, both, provided court physicians in their day. Ellen's brother, John, was to follow family tradition. He was made court physician in 1836.

Uncle Reuben Walker had been the only JP in a district comprising Leeds Bradford, Huddersfield and Halifax during the time of the Luddite riots.

Lovers of *Jane Eyre* will recognise here the "proportions not vast, though considerable; a gentleman's manor house, not a nobleman's seat; battlements round the top (that) give it a picturesque look". There were also grottos, waterfalls and fishponds and woods where bluebells and starwort grew. Sometimes rare birds were shot in the woods.

Once, when Charlotte was staying there, a chestnut tree in the orchard hedge was struck by lightning and thrown to the ground. Charlotte used this incident, too, in *Jane Eyre*. Later, at the end of the book, when Charlotte comes home to find Mr. Rochester blind and crippled, he cries out in his anguish that he "is no better than the old lightning-struck chestnut-tree in Thornfield orchard".

The name *Thornfield* may have come from the tall double hawthorn bushes, red and white, that grew in the park.

Ellen Nussey was Charlotte's closest friend. She had no literary pretensions, but she was to awaken a passionate affection in Charlotte. Charlotte's family liked her, too. "Emily and Anne say they never saw anyone they liked so well as Miss Nussey, " Charlotte wrote from Haworth after Ellen's first visit.

Their affection was well placed for Ellen was loyal to the end. She was with Charlotte when Anne died at Scarborough. "Be a sister in my stead," Anne said to her just before she died. At Charlotte's wedding Ellen was the only bridesmaid.

Pictures of Ellen show her delicate and pretty as a schoolgirl, composed and beautiful in her old age.

In 1837 Ellen Nussey moved from Rydings to Brookroyd House in Brookroyd Lane, Birstall. Charlotte visited Brookroyd many times, sometimes coming by gig, sometimes by train. It was in the grounds of Brookroyd House that she quietly corrected proofs of *Jane Eyre*.

Long afterwards Ellen moved to Moor Lane House, Gomersal, now the Gomersal Park Hotel. She died there on 26 November 1897, at the age of 80 and is buried in Birstall churchyard, east of the church.

Birstall church is Briarfield in *Shirley*. A prehistoric trackway once ran near the site of the church, crossing the beck by a ford. That was long before the church was built.

The present church is not the one Charlotte knew. Like Hartshead, Thornton and Haworth, Birstall Parish Church was rebuilt in the second half of the nineteenth century - in 1866 to be precise, eleven years after Charlotte's death.

But this is where the Revd Matthewson Helstone of *Shirley* was vicar with the Revd Peter Augustus Malone for curate. Their fellow clerics were Dr. Boultby of Whinbury (Dewsbury) with Mr. Donne for curate, and the Revd Cyril Hall of Nunnely (Hartshead) whose curate was the Revd David Sweeting. The prototype for the Revd Cyril Hall was said to have been the Revd William Margetson Heald, Vicar of Birstall, Hon. Canon of Ripon, or his father, or both of them together. Mr. Heald's father, also a Revd William Margetson Heald, had been born at Heald's House, Dewsbury Moor, where later Miss Wooler kept her school.

There is an unusual monument in Birstall Church. It is to the memory of John Nelson, a stone mason, one of

Wesley's faithful lay-evangelist preachers. He suffered for his faith. Arrested, though innocent, thrown into the old Bradford gaol in Ivegate, impressed into the army, he yet survived to come back and help build the Wesleyan Chapel in 1750. He also erected a little hut in the Chapel yard, which is still there. It has a stone over the mantelpiece inscribed, "John Nelson's Study, A.D.1751". Near the hut is a sundial which he also made.

Charlotte must have seen these.

Oakwell Hall (Fieldhead in *Shirley*) is about half a mile from Birstall Church. Charlotte would visit it with Ellen.

Oakwell Hall was built in 1583, five years before the Spanish Armada sailed against Britain. It was built by John Batt and is an almost perfect moated Elizabethan manor house. It was built on the site of an older, timber-framed house, but nothing of this can be seen now. John Batt must have rebuilt completely and he built in stone. There are timber structures inside the house, but, according to tree-ring dating, these are of the 1580 period; not earlier.

There is a mystery at Oakwell. Evidence in the park suggests there was once a small, medieval village there of which nothing remains. No one knows exactly when it existed: whether it crumbled, or was cleared away by the first building of Oakwell Hall, or deserted during plague years. The remains of this village were discovered by archaeological surveying methods, using theodolites and measuring poles which pinpointed, not houses, but the platforms on which these early houses stood. Recently, the same experiment was repeated but this time using electronic measuring equipment and the results obtained by the earlier method were verified

A Batt was still living at Oakwell Hall at the time of the Civil Wars. Captain John Batt did fight for his King, but there is no documentary evidence to show whether he was present at the Battle of Adwalton, or not, even though the fighting took place (on 30 June 1643) no more than a mile from his home.

This battle between the Royalists under the Earl of Newcastle and the Parliamentarians under Lord Fairfax, together with his son, Sir Thomas Fairfax, who had led his men out from Bradford, was one of the important battles of the war. The Parliamentarians were defeated. They were cut off from their base. Those who survived could flee only by going forwards, past Oakwell Hall, down to Birstall Church, up the hill to Gomersal, on to Cleckheaton, Bailiff Bridge and Halifax. The next day some returned by a round-about route to Bradford, only to leave again as soon as possible because of the Royalists. The Earl of Newcastle made Bolling Hall his headquarters.

When the Parliamentarians eventually came to power John Batt was fined £364 for resisting their cause. This was one tenth of his estate.

Charlotte must have known Oakwell Hall well. In *Shirley* she described it both inside and out. Early in Chapter II she wrote, "you could see a high gable, then a long front, then a low gable; then a thick, lofty stack of chimneys; there were some trees behind it". Inside she described the oak-panelled drawing-room (the great parlour) that some "benevolent barbarian" had colour-washed "pinky white". And Charlotte approved! "Very handsome, reader, these shining brown panels are: very mellow in colouring and tasteful in effect, but - if you know what a 'Spring clean' is - very execrable and inhuman".

I suppose it is 'excerable and inhuman' again, now, although nobody seems to grumble. The pinky-white colour-wash has been stripped off to reveal painted and patterned panelling, almost too ornamental, baffling the eyes. There is another similarly-panelled room upstairs. The panelling is not as it was when first put in *c.*1583, when the house was built. The panels were painted about a hundred years later, probably because by that time small panels were no longer fashionable and the painting was an attempt to reflect contemporary style. What a pity Chrlotte did not know about this; one can imagine her wry laughter.

But it was in the parlour, to the right of the entrance, the "brown-panelled parlour" that Caroline Helstone (brought by her uncle, the Revd Matthewson Helstone, to meet Shirley Keeldar) found a middle-aged, somewhat eccentric lady called Mrs. Pryor. Mrs. Pryor had been Shirley's governess, but was now her friend. She also turned out to be Caroline's long lost mother. The second half of *Shirley* was written after Charlotte had lost Branwell, Emily and Anne all within twelve months, and the scenes where Caroline realises who Mrs. Pryor really is, and where she accepts her as her mother, move one almost to tears. Charlotte never knew what it was to have a mother.

In the hall there are 'dog-gates' at the foot of the stairs, put there to keep dogs from the balcony above and from the bedrooms; but the 'dog-gates' failed to keep two curates from the bedrooms in an hilarious scene after they had struck Tartar, Shirley's dog.

*The dog made a spring: the second gentleman turned tail and rushed after his comrade: the first was already safe in a bedroom:*

*Oakwell Hall*

*"Gentlemen!" Shirley admonished them: "... that is Mrs. Pryor's apartment."*

*Only little Mr. Sweeting, coming later, was not upset by Tartar. "What - Tartar, Tartar!" said a cheery, rather boyish voice: "don't you know us? Good-morning, old boy!"*

Another interesting part of Oakwell Hall is the dairy at the back of the house. There is a sign "DIRY" over the window. In William III's reign money had become so worn and clipped that it was decided to demonetize all the old coins and replace them. This great recoinage cost the country £2,000,000. The money to pay was raised by the imposition of a "window-tax". House owners had to pay so much for each window they possessed. (It was a kind of income-tax) That is why one can often see windows blocked up in old houses. They were then exempt from tax. Other exemptions were dairy windows and cheese-room windows, which were to be wholly without glass. They were also to have the words "Dairy" or "Cheese-room" carved or clearly painted on them. This tax lasted - as taxes do - from 1696 to 1851.

What was it, one wonders, that brought Charlotte Brontë to Oakwell Hall so often that she knew it inside and out, upstairs and down? By the time of Charlotte's first visit to Rydings after leaving Roe Head in 1832, Oakwell Hall was a boarding school for girls. Later, by 1838, the school had been taken over by the Cockills - mother and three daughters - and one of those daughters, Elizabeth, had been a pupil at Roe Head School when Charlotte and Ellen and Mary Taylor were also there. They liked each other and formed what would nowadays be called a social network of which Charlotte, on her visits to both Ellen and Mary, would be a welcome part. All of them were teachers. It is often forgotten that Ellen, herself, taught in Sunday Schools for many years, gaining practical experience and probably teaching more subjects than scripture. Years after Charlotte's death, when the Miss Carters took over Oakwell, she did some teaching there, and in the village school at Birstall as well; so she, too, would be caught up in Charlotte's dream of running a school, like Oakwell Hall and Miss Wooler's, in which Charlotte's sisters, Emily and Anne, would find a place and be able to stay at home together with herself, Branwell and their ageing father.

This was not to be. Branwell, Emily and Anne all died and the dream of a school came to nothing; Oakwell Hall, however, was transformed into "Fieldhead", the home of Shirley Keelder in Charlotte's novel *Shirley* and was immortalised; but the story of Oakwell Hall has not ended yet. It is now displayed as a Period House of the late seventeenth century and is open to the public. It is also very well used by educational groups that benefit from its award winning programmes linked to the new National Curriculum.

# An Age of Governesses

William Scruton in his *Pen and Pencil Pictures of Old Bradford*, published in 1889, recorded the following memory of the Brontë sisters.

> *... an old Bradfordian yet living (he wrote) who knew them well both before they became famous and after, wrote thus; - "I have seen the Brontë sisters many, times. They were the most timid and sensitive creatures it was possible to gaze upon. They generally dressed in old-fashioned gowns of faded black silk, whilst their feet were encased in strong low-fitting shoes and various hued stockings. If you met them in Kirkgate or any other narrow street on a Thursday or a Saturday, when throngs of people were about, they invariably clung to the wall fast hold of each other, as if afraid of being noticed. They were the shyest ladies, too, I ever knew, principally accounted for, no doubt, by their short-sightedness, their not inter-mixing with general society, and by their living in such an outlandish place as Haworth. Little did the people of Bradford, who gazed with such curiosity on Patrick Brontë's daughters, imagine that they were to play so prominent a part in the literary world".*

Such were the three whom circumstances forced to become governesses!

Even today, anyone who wishes to earn money must go where the work is. By 1836, when Charlotte was twenty, a new, rich, but very uneducated social class had come into being - the successful mill-owners. These men and women had risen in the world. They had money, but were deficient in many of the things that went towards the making of gentlemen and gentlewomen and they were intelligent enough to know it. They wanted their children to have a better chance in life than they themselves had had, so they engaged governesses, but, having little learning themselves, they were not able to appreciate culture. They were patronising towards what they thought money could buy easily.

It is understandable that the Brontë sisters were unhappy in these homes. The vicarages of England furnished many such people at that time, equal in suffering, if inarticulate.

The places where the sisters worked that are near enough to be included in a pilgrimage centred on the Spen Valley, are Heald's House, Dewsbury Moor and Upperwood House, Rawdon, where Charlotte taught, Law Hill, Southowram, Halifax, the scene of Emily's sole teaching venture, and the Blake Hall Drive Estate, Mirfield, where Blake Hall once stood and where Anne took up her first post.

Charlotte took her first teaching post at Miss Wooler's school (Roe Head and Heald's House) mainly to enable Branwell to study painting at the Royal Academy School, London, although also to pay for board and tuition for Emily and then Anne. She was to keep the position for three years. Her salary was £16 per annum.

Charlotte was not unused to children or to teaching for she had taught (as Caroline was to do in *Shirley*) in the

Sunday School at home. But this was sheer drudgery. Charlotte had hoped to save a little. She found that was impossible.

Worse still, in spite of all her sacrifice, Branwell, who had gone to London with high hopes and letters of introduction in his pocket, came back penniless and despairing. He had never even presented those letters. He was beaten before he started. He never did make the grade.

The wonder is that Charlotte stayed at Miss Wooler's as long as she did, before ill health drove her home.

It was while Charlotte was at Miss Wooler's that Emily tried her fortune at Law Hill.

Law Hill is still standing - at Southowram, 2½ miles south-east of Halifax. It is a solid, stone building, erected in 1771 by a thoroughly unscrupulous character called Jack Sharpe. It was opened as a school in 1825, twelve years before Emily arrived. Miss Patchett's Academy was a girl's boarding school. There were 40 pupils.

It was a sheer act of courage that drove Emily to Law Hill after only three months of regular schooling in the whole of her life (excepting, of course, the disastrous period at Cowan Bridge). "I fear she will never stand it," Charlotte wrote. But she did stand it - either for six months or eighteen months; we don't know which. Moreover, fifty years afterwards old ladies, reminiscing over their schooldays there, remembered, "a Miss Brontë" who was "not unpopular", although she did tell one class that she preferred the dog to any of them!

More important still - to us - is the fact that only two miles from Law Hill stood High Sunderland Hall, where friends of Miss Patchett's, the Priestleys, lived. Miss Patchett, a handsome, vivacious woman of forty-five, had antiquarian interests. It would seem she took Emily there one day because Wuthering Heights, especially the principal door, is modelled in part on High Sunderland Hall. Around the entrance of both were the "crumbling griffins and shameless little boys".

The story of Jack Sharpe, too, (adopted by an uncle whom he later swindled) could have contained a germ of *Wuthering Heights* - although the theme was already family property. There was also a servant called Mrs. Earnshaw while Emily was there.

As for Anne's writings, the first half of her novel *Agnes Grey* was based solidly on her experiences at Blake Hall, Mirfield.

Blake Hall is no longer there. The name persists though in the modern housing estate centred on Blake Hall Drive. Blake Hall was erected in 1745, enlarged in 1845 and eventually pulled down in 1954. It is a nice thought that its lovely old staircase was bought (with ghost) by Mr. Topping of Long Island, New York.

Anne arrived on 8 April 1839. She was to be governess to two of the children of Dr. and Mrs. Ingham. Dr. Ingham was descended from Benjamin Ingham (1712-72), the Ossett boy who became the friend of John and Charles Wesley. At the time Anne arrived they had five children. Later the number increased to thirteen.

It was disastrous for the Inghams' reputation that there came a child among them, taking notes. Anne Brontë's description of the behaviour of those children is beyond belief. Against this one must remember that this was Anne's first teaching post. She had had no experience of handling children and, as any teacher knows, even the best children sense weakness immediately and take advantage.

Like the heroine of her novel Anne was eventually dismissed, but she left undefeated in spirit, determined to try again somewhere else and do better. This she did. She was the only one of the sisters who really made a success of teaching.

Charlotte's last situation was at Upperwood House, Rawdon. Upperwood House, too, has been pulled down, but a fine new house, "Brontë House", has been built in the grounds that Charlotte knew and admired.

Upperwood House was very near Woodhouse Grove School where Patrick Brontë met Maria Branwell. Brontë House is now - appropriately - a preparatory department for Woodhouse Grove School.

Charlotte was twenty-five when she went there. She was, by this time, an experienced teacher and her employers, Mr. and Mrs. White, were hospitable. Mr. White urged Mr. Brontë to spend a week with them. Even Charlotte said that they were "kind people in their way".

Yet she admitted, "home-sickness afflicts me sorely," and also "it is dreary, solitary work".

Nevertheless it was at Upperwood House that a new dream was born, a dream that was to alter Charlotte's whole life. Mary Taylor wrote to her there from Brussels. Her letter awakened in Charlotte "an urgent thirst to see - to know - to learn". Charlotte found herself longing to go to school again as a pupil, this time in Brussels.

The Whites encouraged her.

When Charlotte left Upperwood House it was with real regret on both sides. "They only made too much of me", Charlotte said. "I did not deserve it".

Perhaps they understood her better than she realised.

# Shirley

This, then, is the Spen Valley and its environs - the countryside, the people and the events that contributed to the creation of *Shirley. Shirley* however is much more than that.

When Charlotte started to write *Shirley* her family - her two sisters and one brother - were all alive and reasonably well, but increasingly Branwell's health and mental stability failed. Something of the bewilderment and terror the family felt, watching his disintegration, is reflected in *Shirley*, in Mrs. Pryor's memories of her husband, Caroline's father. When the book was only half written, Branwell died - on 24 September 1848. Three months later , 19 December 1848, Emily died. Five months later 28 May 1849, Anne died.

It was impossible to sick nurse and write a novel at the same time. The book was put away. When Charlotte took up her pen again and started to write, she called her new chapter *The Valley of the Shadow of Death*. It is significant, too, that in this chapter Charlotte unconsciously changed the colour of Caroline's eyes from brown to blue, as though the concept of her heroine had undergone a change.

Yet this is the one book of all Charlotte's novels that shows Charlotte at her happiest and best. It is not a well constructed novel and the character of the second hero, Louis Moore, is sadly lacking in substance, but there is some fine characterisation in it. The Revd Matthewson Helstone lives and breathes. Hiram Yorke and all his family are firmly rooted in reality. As for Mademoiselle Moore - Robert's and Louis's sister, Hortense - she is the perfect character (in print) to take to a desert island. Charlotte had a wicked sense of humour and used it to good effect in *Shirley*. Remember the curates? Mr. Nicholls's landlady was thoroughly alarmed when he read the book. She heard him "giving vent to roars of laughter as he sat alone, clapping his hands and stamping on the floor". This was the curate, the Revd Mr. Macarthy in *Shirley*, whom Charlotte married!

It is heartening to remember that it was the writing of *Shirley* that helped pull Charlotte through her own Valley of the Shadow of Death to her short-lived, but very real happiness with her husband, the Revd Arthur Bell Nicholls.

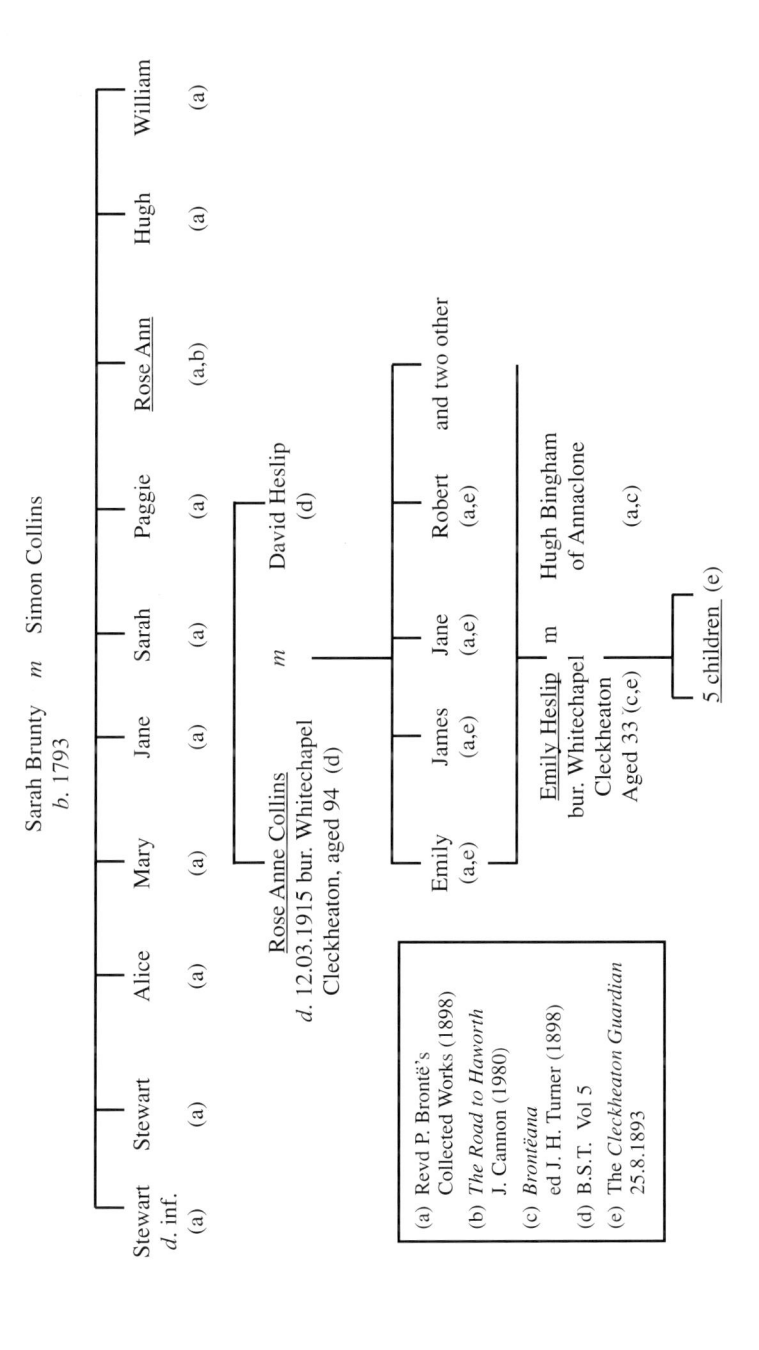

Sarah Brunty  *m*  Simon Collins
b. 1793

| Stewart | Stewart | Alice | Mary | Jane | Sarah | Paggie | Rose Ann | Hugh | William |
|---|---|---|---|---|---|---|---|---|---|
| d. inf. | (a) | (a) | (a) | (a) | (a) | (a) | (a,b) | (a) | (a) |
| (a) | | | | | | | | | |

Rose Anne Collins   *m*   David Heslip
d. 12.03.1915 bur. Whitechapel                (d)
Cleckheaton, aged 94 (d)

| Emily | James | Jane | Robert | and two other |
|---|---|---|---|---|
| (a,e) | (a,e) | (a,e) | (a,e) | |

Emily Heslip   m   Hugh Bingham
bur. Whitechapel            of Annaclone
Cleckheaton
Aged 33 (c,e)                  (a,c)

5 children (e)

(a) Revd P. Brontë's
    Collected Works (1898)
(b) *The Road to Haworth*
    J. Cannon (1980)
(c) *Brontëana*
    ed J. H. Turner (1898)
(d) B.S.T. Vol 5
(e) The *Cleckheaton Guardian*
    25.8.1893

87

# Postscript
## Charlotte Brontë's Cousin : Rose Ann Heslip

Monday, 15 March 1915! A tiny, but significant group of people gathered at Whitechapel, Cleckheaton for the funeral of Mrs. Rose Ann Heslip who had died three days earlier, aged 94. Present, besides her son-in-law and grandchildren, were Mr. John James Stead of Heckmondwike and Mrs. Lumb of Triangle, near Halifax, Yorkshire, both representatives of the Brontë Society. The well-known author and editor Mr. J. Horsfall Turner of Idle, Bradford was also one of the mourners, for Mrs. Heslip was the last of the Brontë family to be laid to rest in Yorkshire soil. She was the Revd Patrick Brontë's niece and his children's cousin; yet they had never met and the only echo of her existence that has come to us through them was from Charlotte who once mentioned an "Aunt Collins" to Ellen Nussey, of whom she said she knew little, to her regret. That, of course, was long before Mrs. Heslip (née Collins) came to live in the Spen Valley.

Mrs. Heslip's mother was born Sarah Brunty (Brontë) and she was Patrick's sister. He had five sisters and four brothers. Sarah, a twin, was the only girl who married although two of Patrick's brothers did. Sarah married Simon Collins and they had ten children, all born in Ireland. Strangely, of the ten, Rose Ann Collins was the only one to marry and carry on the line.

Rose Ann was born in 1821. She spent the early part of her life in the vicinity of the old homestead at Ballynashkeagh, Co. Down and worked for her Uncle Hugh. She always spoke with pride of her mother and others of that generation, insisting on their good looks and especially on their robust health, so strangely different from the health of the generation that followed. Patrick, she remembered, had always been ambitious and anxious to escape into the greater world. When, at last, he started his journey to England "he did not follow the circuitous roads, but went as the crow flies over hedge and ditch".

It was a longer journey that brought Mrs. Heslip to Yorkshire. While still in Ireland she married David Heslip and, according to the *Cleckheaton Guardian*, 25 August 1893, she had six children, all of whom died of the same disease to which the Brontë sisters succumbed - consumption. Only Emily, of all the six children, lived to marry and bear children herself. She married Hugh Bingham of Annaclone and they had five children. Emily and Hugh moved to Irvine, in Scotland, and it was there that Emily fell ill and Mrs. Heslip left her Irish home to nurse her. Times were harsh and the family drifted south in search of work, ending up at Salthorn at the top end of the Spen Valley beyond Oakenshaw and now just inside the Bradford boundary, where Hugh became foreman at a near-by gasworks. Here, in their new home, Emily died aged 33 and was buried at Whitechapel. Her mother stayed on to look after her son-in-law and her grandchildren.

After the green fields of Ireland Salthorn must have broken her heart. "Some 30 or 40 years ago", the *Heckmondwike Herald* of 24 August 1893 reports:

> *Salthorn was a deserted, forlorn place, surrounded by black pit-hills and standing amidst swamps and pools on the rough uncultivated common - at night lighted up by the lurid flames which belch from the furnaces at Low Moor and Bowling. The place has had the reputation ... of*

> *furnishing a higher proportion of suicides than any other place in the locality but ... a fair number of new cottages now surround the old inn from which the village seems to take its name.*

The story of how Mrs. Heslip was *found* by the literary world is one worthy of the Brontës. The family in Ireland, of course, knew of their writing for copies of each book were duly sent over, probably by Patrick who also helped his family with gifts of money. Family ties were never broken; indeed, two of Patrick's brothers Uncle James and Uncle Hugh, both, visited Haworth and were treated royally - Hugh was brought to Kirklees to see Robin Hood's grave - and both reported back their impressions of the children. Uncle James said Charlotte was "very inquisitive and wanted a heap of news". He added that she "had a very wee foot and was sighted" - he meant she had bad eyesight - "but," he added, "her eyes were as clear as diamonds". He was puzzled by Anne who wanted to go home with him when he left. She called Ireland "home".

Consequently, when the Revd William Wright, D.D., a literary investigator, wrote about the Brontës in Ireland in *McClure's Magazine*, and extracts were republished in the *Bradford Daily Telegraph*, Mrs. Heslip read them and was displeased! She considered certain parts were deeply insulting. Dr. Wright had made her family (and Patrick's) appear rude and simple and she was not having it, so she sent her son-in-law, Hugh Bingham, to London to discover the author of these scurrilous writings! This led to a news interview with Mrs. Heslip who, until then, had been quite unknown. Even the unpopular Dr. Wright called on her eventually and she told him what she thought of him! That was in 1893 when Mrs. Heslip was 72 years of age. It is a great pity that Charlotte Brontë, who died in 1855, did not live to see the day. She would have enjoyed it.

Once the secret was out the press and representatives of the Brontë Society flocked to visit her. Among the visitors was Heckmondwike's John James Stead, who took her photograph. A letter written by him on 3 October 1893 to a friend called Rhodes reads "I don't know whether I told you that after Mr. Peel and myself had been to interview Mrs. Heslip (Charlotte Brontë's cousin) I went a day or two after and took a photo of her - I enclose a copy...." It makes one wonder, did Frank Peel write the description of Salthorn mentioned above? It is written in his style.

*Mrs Rose Heslip*

Shortly after that, on 4 November - and through the kindness of Dr. Wright! - Rose Heslip was taken to Haworth for the very first time. Interestingly, the church was kept locked as most are today, but they used not to be, and the caretaker brought the key and took the party round. Afterwards she spoke of Mrs. Heslip's "likeness to Charlotte". Probably she was like Charlotte in character too, for she stooped over the brass family memorial and murmured, "I am glad it is only the names!". Then she was taken to the Black Bull where, like so many other pilgrims, she sat in Branwell's chair. There is no mention that she visited the Parsonage. Later she remarked that it must have been a sad and lonely life for her relatives and that if Branwell was like his Irish ancestors there was little wonder that he went astray, for they demanded a full life without monotony and peopled with human beings and interwoven with companionships. This was probably a commentary on her own life, too.

Yet she had courage. She had named her only daughter Emily after Emily Brontë and her thoughts must have been on both as she watched her own child dying of consumption. She lived another 22 years after her daughter's death. Her final comment on her cousins' books was that she "did not agree with their sad tone and preferred a more cheerful view of life".

The reporter, writing in the *Heckmondwike Herald* of 24 August 1893 commented on the family likeness that had been passed to some of the grandchildren. Without realising it he echoed descriptions of Charlotte Brontë when he wrote of "a little bright-eyed girl who sat in the corner eying us very curiously". If any descendants of that little girl, or her siblings, are still living Brontë enthusiasts would be delighted to hear of them.

# Sources and Bibliography

Barker, Juliet, *The Brontës* Weidenfield and Nicolson, (1994).

Brontë, Charlotte, *Jane Eyre*, Penguin Classics, (1985).

Brontë, Charlotte, *Shirley,* Penguin Classics, (1985).

Brontë, Charlotte, *The Letters of Charlotte Brontë*, edited by Margaret Smith, Volume I 1829-1847, Clarenden Press (Oxford, 1995).

Brontë, Revd Patrick, *Collected Works*, edited by J. Horsfall Turner. (Bingley, 1898).

Gaskell, Mrs. *The Life of Charlotte Brontë,* Everyman's Library, Dent, (1917).

Gerin, Winifred, *Charlotte Brontë,* O.U.P. (1967).

Locke, John and Dixon, Canon W.T., *A Man of Sorrow : the life, letters and times of the Rev. Patrick Brontë, 1777-1861*, Ian Hedgkins & Co. Ltd., (1979).

Peters, Margot, *Unquiet Soul*, Hodder and Stoughton, (1975).

Taylor, Mary, *Letters from New Zealand and Elsewhere*, edited by Joan Stevens, Auckland University Press and OUP, (1972).

Whitehead, Barbara, *Charlotte Brontë and her 'dearest Nell'*, Smith Settle (Otley, Yorkshire, 1993).

# Brontë Society Transactions

Clapham, Barbara, *Charlotte Brontë and Oakwell Hall,* (B.S.T, 1978).

Hatfield, C.W. and Edgerley, C M, *The Relatives of Miss Ellen Nussey*, (BST, 1939).

Holgate, Ivy, *The Brontës at Thornton* (B.S.T., 1959)

Holgate, Ivy, *The Cottage in the Wood* (B.S.T., 1957)

Nussey, Ellen, *Reminiscences of Charlotte Brontë* (B.S.T. 1906)

Wilson, Hon. Lady, *The Brontës as Governesses*, (BST, 1939)

# History and Social background

Clark, Sir George, *The Later Stuarts*, OUP (1964)

Collingwood, W.G., *Northumbrian Crosses of the Pre- Norman Age*, Faber & Gwyer (1927)

Collingwood, W.G., *Angles, Danes and Norse in the District of Huddersfield*, Tolson Memorial Museum, (Huddersfield, 1929)

Faull, M.L. and Moorhouse, S.A., editors, *West Yorkshire: an archaeological survey to A.D.1500*. West Yorkshire Metropolitan County Council (1981)

Holt, J.C., *Robin Hood*, Thames & Hudson Ltd, (1982)

Leadley, Tom, *Lee Fair : the story of England's oldest Charter Fair*, Tom Leadley, (West Ardsley, Wakefield 1994).

Peel, Frank, *The Risings of the Luddites*, John Hartley "Echo Offices" (Dewsbury, 1895)

*Proceedings of the York Special Commission, January 1813* (second edition) London. Printed by Luke Hansard and Sons near Lincoln's Inn Fields.

Reid, Robert, *Land of Lost Content : the Luddite Revolt*, 1812, Heinemann, (1986), Sphere Books (1988)

Rose, Martial, Ed.. *The Wakefield Mystery Plays*, Evans Brothers Ltd., (1961)

Spen Valley Historical Society Journal, (1988).

Thomis, Malcolm, *The Luddites* David & Charles (1970)

Wedgwood, C.V., *The King's War*, 1641-1647, Collins Fontana Library (1966).

Wright, Thomas, Ed., *Autobiography of Joseph Lister of Bradford 1627-1709 John Russell Smith (1842)*

# Topographical

Cadman, H. Ashwell, *Gomersal Past and Present*, Hunters Armley Ltd. (Leeds 1930)

Cradock, H.C., *A History of the Ancient Parish of Birstall*, SPCK, (1933)

Cudworth, William, *Round about Bradford*, Thomas Brear, (Bradford 1876)

James, John, *The History and Topography of Bradford*, Longman, Brown, Green and Longmans: and Charles Stansfield, (Bradford MDCCCXLI, Centenary edition 1967)

Pobjoy, H.N., *History of Mirfield,* The Ridings Publishing Company, (Driffield, Yorkshire, 1969)

Scruton, William, *Pen & pencil pictures of Old Bradford*, Thomas Brear & Co. Ltd., (Bradford 1889)

Scruton, William, *Thornton and the Brontës* John Dale & Co. Ltd., (Bradford 1898)

Stuart, J.A. Erskin, *The Brontë Country,* Longmans, Green & Co., (London 1888)

Stuart, J.A. Erskin, *The Literary Shrines of Yorkshire*, (London 1892)

Whitehead, Phyllis *The Brontës came here*, Fawcett Greenwood & Co Ltd., (Halifax)

Wright, Thomas, *Autobiography of Thomas Wright of Birkenshaw, 1736-1797. Edited* by his grandson Thomas Wright, John Russell Smith, (1864).

*Heckmondwike Herald*     24.08.1893
*The Cleckheaton Guardian*     24.08.1893

Red House, Gomersal
Oakwell Hall, Birstall

The Taylor Graves in Firdene Wood, Gomersal
Holly Bank School (Mirfield) Prospectus

# Places and People

| | | |
|---|---|---|
| Birstall | Briarfield | *Shirley* |
| Birstall Church | Briarfield Church | *Shirley* |
| Blake Hall | Wellwood | *Agnes Grey* |
| Dewsbury | Whinbury | *Shirley* |
| Hartshead | Nunnely | *Shirley* |
| Hartshead Church | Nunnely Church | *Shirley* |
| High Sunderland Hall (with High Withens, nr. Haworth) | Wuthering Heights | *Wuthering Heights* |
| Hunsworth Mill (with Rawfolds Mill) | Hollows Mill | *Shirley* |
| Kirklees Park | Nunnwood | *Shirley* |
| Kirklees Hall | Home of Sir Philip Nunnely | *Shirley* |
| Oakwell Hall | Fieldhead | *Shirley* |
| Rawfolds Mill (with Hunsworth Mill) | Hollows Mill | *Shirley* |
| Red House | Briarmains | *Shirley* |
| Rydings | Thornfield Hall | *Jane Eyre* |
| Cartwright, William | Robert Moore | *Shirley* |
| Heald, Revd William Margetson (father) | Revd Cyril Hall | *Shirley* |
| Heald, Revd William Margetson (son) | Revd Cyril Hall | *Shirley* |
| Nussey, Ellen | Caroline Helstone | *Shirley* |
| Nussey, Henry | St. John Rivers | *Jane Eyre* |
| Roberson, Revd Hammond | Revd Matthewson Helstone | *Shirley* |
| Taylor, Anne (Mary's mother) | Mrs. Yorke | *Shirley* |
| Taylor, Joshua (Mary's father) | Hiram Yorke | *Shirley* |
| Taylor, Joshua (Mary's brother) | Matthew Yorke | *Shirley* |
| Taylor, Martha (Mary's sister) | Jessie Yorke | *Shirley* |
| Taylor, Mary | Rose Yorke | *Shirley* |
| Wooler, Margaret | Mrs. Pryor | *Shirley* |

**Shirley, of course, was Emily Brontë**

# Index

## A

Act of Uniformity  32
Adwalton, Battle of  33, 75
Agnes Grey  83
Anglo-Saxons  3, 19
Armytage, Sir John  21
Atkinson, Revd Thomas  5, 30-31, 57
Aunt Collins  88

## B

Bingham, Hugh  89, 90
Birkenshaw  62
Birstall  46, 70, 73
Birstall Parish Church  73, 74, 75
Blake Hall, Mirfield  81, 83
Bonnell Collection  45
Booth, John  54
Bradford  1, 32, 39, 88, 89
Branwell, Miss  37, 38
Brontë, Anne  35, 44-46, 72, 76, 79, 81, 83, 84, 85, 90
Brontë, Branwell  35, 44, 70, 76, 81, 82, 85, 92
Brontë, Charlotte  2, 3, 7, 11, 22-24, 27, 29, 31, 35, 37-46, 51, 52, 54, 60-64, 66-70, 72-79, 81, 82, 84-86, 88, 90-92
Brontë, Elizabeth  29, 30, 35
Brontë, Emily  35, 44, 76, 79, 81-83, 85, 92
Brontë, Maria  (née Branwell; Patrick's wife)  28, 29, 32-37, 84
Brontë, Maria  (Patrick's daughter)  29, 30
Brontë Parsonage Museum  45
Brontë, Patrick  1-3, 5-9, 11, 12, 15-18, 20-23, 28-39, 43, 46, 56-58, 84, 88-90
Brontë Society  88, 91
Brontë, Uncle Hugh  90
Brontë, Uncle James  90
Brookroyd House  73
Brunty, Sarah  88
Brussels  85
Buckworth, Revd John  5, 8, 11, 12, 16
Butterfield, Francis  39

## C

Cadman, H.Ashwell  65
Carrett, Elliot  5
Cartwright, William  48, 50, 51, 54, 55, 57
Cartwright's Mill  (Rawfold's Mill)  39, 43, 48-51, 54, 55, 57, 58
Castle Hill, Almondbury  17
Chartist movement  39
Cleckheaton  1, 19
Clough Lane, Hightown  29, 30
Cockill, family  78
Conventicle Act  33
*Cottage in the Wood*  22, 38
*Cottage Poems*  22, 38
Cowan Bridge  1, 30, 38, 82
Croppers  47-48
Cropping machine  47-48
Cudworth, William  33

## D

Dewsbury  1-16, 19
Dewsbury Cutting  10
Dewsbury Minster  2, 3, 5
Dumb Steeple  24, 49

## E

Earlsheaton  10, 11
Elmet, Kingdom of  19

## F

Fennell, Jane  28, 29
Firdene Wood  65, 66
Firth, Dr.  37
Firth, Elizabeth  37,  38

## G

Garrs, Nancy  37
Gaskell, Mrs.  17, 32, 43, 70
Gawthorpe  11
Gomersal Bank  66
Gomersal Churchyard  68
Guiseley  28

## H

Halliley, Mr.  16
Hartshead  16, 17-23, 28-32
Hartshead Moor  19, 48
Haworth  39
Heald, Revd William Margetson  73
Heald's Hall, Liversedge  56
Heald's House, Dewsbury  45,  81
Heckmondwike  1
Heslip, Emily,  89
Heslip, Rose Ann  88-92
High Royd  67
High Sunderland Hall  83
Hightown  29, 30
Hirst, John  58
Holgate, Mrs. Ivy  38
Holly Bank School  40
Holt, J.C.  24
Hunsworth  1, 62-63
Hunsworth Mill  62-63

## I

Industrial Revolution  47
Ingham, Dr.  83

## J

*Jane Eyre*  22, 31, 67, 72

## K

Kaye, Benjamin  38
Kaye, Mercy  38
Kipping  33
Kirklees Gatehouse  25, 26
Kirklees Hall  21, 23, 90
Kirklees Priory  23, 27
Kirkstall Abbey  28
Knowles, Herbert  68

## L

Latter Lee Fair  12-14
Law Hill, Southowram, Halifax  81, 82
Lee Fair  13
Lister, Accepted  33
Lister, Joseph  33
Little John  25
Liversedge  39, 58
Liversedge Church  43, 56, 57
Luddites  39, 48-51, 54-55, 57-59, 67, 71

## M

*Maid of Killarney*  22, 38
Miss Miles  40, 67
Miss Patchett's Academy  82
Molyneaux, Charles  55
Moor Lane House, Gomersal  73
Morgan, William  28, 29, 43

## N

Nelson, John  73, 74
New Zealand  63, 66, 67
Nicholls, Revd Arthur Bell  70, 86
Nonconformists  33
Nostell Priory  12, 13
Nowell, William  12, 14, 15
Nussey, Ellen  40-46, 63, 66, 70-73, 78-79, 88

## O

Oakenshaw  89
Oakwell Hall  74-79

## P

Palmerston, Lord  15
Peel, Frank  51, 91
Pevsner, Nikolaus,  26
Pollard Hall  68
Power looms  39

## R

Ravensthorpe  1
Rawfolds Mill  43, 48-51, 57
Red House  60-68
River Calder  1, 3, 9, 17, 19
River Spen  1, 19, 50
Roberson, Revd Hammond  5, 7, 8, 43, 54, 56-57
Robin Hood  23-27, 90
Roe Head  2, 31, 40-44, 49, 78, 81
Romans  19
*Rural Minstrel*  22
Rydings  70-72

## S

Saint Paulinus  3
Salthorn  89
Scarborough  72
Scruton, William  39, 80
Shillicake Wood  38
*Shirley*  7, 11, 23, 27, 29, 39, 46, 51, 60-64, 66, 67, 73-79, 81, 85, 86
Southey, Robert  68, 69
Spen Valley  1, 47, 85, 88
Spenborough  1
Squirrel Hall, Dewsbury  56
Star Inn, Roberttown  54
Starkey, James  58
Stead, James John  88, 91
Sunday Schools  7, 8, 21, 56, 79

## T

Taylor, John  (Mary's grandfather) 62, 64, 65
Taylor, John (Mary's brother)  63
Taylor, Joseph  63
Taylor, Joshua (Mary's father)  61-62, 65-67
Taylor, Joshua (Mary's brother) 65, 66
Taylor, Mary  40, 45, 60-67, 85
Taylor, Richard Waring  65
Thackray, James  14, 15
Thorn Bush Farm  22
Thornton  32-39
Thornton Church  35
Tighe, Revd Thomas  7
Townend, Simeon  39
Turner, J Horsfall  88

## U

Upperwood House, Rawdon  81, 84, 85

## W

Wakefield Mystery Plays  13
Walker, Reuben  71
Walton Cross  19, 20
Wesley, John  7, 64
White Lee Jail  64
Whitechapel, Cleckheaton  88, 89
Whitsuntide Sing  10, 11
Woodhouse Grove School  28, 84
Woodkirk  12
Woodkirk Fair  13
Wooler, Miss Margaret  2, 41-46
Wright, Revd William  90, 92
Wright, Thomas  62
*Wuthering Heights*  83

## Y

Yates, W.W.  6, 11
Yew Tree Inn  54
York Special Commission  58

# Notes

# Notes

A life Member of the Brontë Society, Mabel Ferrett lives in the heart of the countryside she describes. She is the Founder President of the Spen Valley Historical Society.

She is the author of an historical novel, *The Angry Men* (about the Chartists) published by E. J. Arnold and Sons Ltd. Leeds, which was serialised for radio by Olive Shapley and broadcast in three installments on Radio 4 in 1967 and 1968; also *The Taylors of the Red House*, published by Kirklees Leisure Services, Libraries, Museums and Arts Division in 1987.

In 1996 Salzburg University published a substantial collection of her poetry under the title *Scathed Earth*.